We Pledge Our Hearts

We Pledge Our Hearts

*A Treasury of Poems, Quotations and Readings
to Celebrate Love and Marriage*

COLLECTED BY EDWARD SEARL

Skinner House Books
Boston

ISBN 1-55896-503-3
978-1-55896-503-4

Printed in the United States

Cover art *Centering*, © 2002 Eleanor Rubin, http://ellyrubinjournal. typepad.com

09 08 07 06
6 5 4 3 2 1

We gratefully acknowledge permission to reprint copyrighted materials starting on page 183.

Library of Congress Cataloging-in-Publication Data

We pledge our hearts : a treasury of poems, quotations, and readings to celebrate love and marriage / collected by Edward Searl.
    p. cm.
  Includes index.
  ISBN-13: 978-1-55896-503-4 (pbk. : alk. paper)
  ISBN-10: 1-55896-503-3 (pbk. : alk. paper) 1. Love—Literary collections. 2. Marriage—Literary collections. I. Searl, Edward, 1947-

PN6071.L7W4 2006
808.8'03543--dc22

2006010738

Contents

Dear Reader,

Falling in love is a peak experience—fiercely private but nevertheless universal. Over time, love becomes a matter of faith. It takes trust and will for two people to stay together, to work out difficulties, to lean on each other for support, and to open to each other fully. We celebrate commitment for its strength, courage, hope, patience, and constancy. Love and marriage remake our world through the togetherness of each couple, in every day of their relationship.

These poems, quotations, and readings are offered to inform and hearten you on the day of your wedding or commitment ceremony, your golden anniversary, or any day. The writing collected here gives voice to love's many expressions—from an enchanted first glance and the throes of early passion, through the hard work of trusting and sharing, to a sure intimation of the divine. In these selections I hope you will recognize your love, whether it is brand new or long-standing.

Like love itself, these readings span the ages. The authors represent a variety of personal perspectives and cultures. Taken as a whole, the collection illuminates the universality of love and commitment. I hope, indeed anticipate, that you will find in this book ample inspiration to enhance your own ability to love. And for you who have taken, or are about to take, that great leap of faith with a partner, I hope these carefully chosen words will allow you to better appreciate the great journey that you are beginning.

Wishing you love and fulfillment,

Edward Searl

Love Is the Only Magic

Merlin Said

Love is the only magic.

It enriches the giver
    as it nourishes the object.
It serves the instant
    and washes over the ages.
It is as particular as the moon
    and as universal as the heavens. If
returned it is multiplied,
    yet spurned it is not diminished. It
is as lusty as the rutting stag
    but chaste as the unicorn's pillow.
It comes alike to the king on his throne
    and the cutpurse in the market. If
you would have magic,
    place faith in love or nothing.

PATRICK MURFIN

When all the people of the world love,
Then the strong will not overpower the weak.
The many will not oppress the few.
The wealthy will not mock the poor.
The honored will not disdain the humble.
The cunning will not deceive the simple.

MO-TSE

A thought transfixed me: for the first time in my life I saw the truth as it is set into song by so many poets, proclaimed as the final wisdom by so many thinkers. The truth—that love is the ultimate and the highest goal to which man can aspire. Then I grasped the meaning of the greatest secret that human poetry and human thought and belief have to impart: *The salvation of man is through love and in love.* I understood how a man who has nothing left in this world still may know bliss, be it only for a brief moment, in the contemplation of his beloved. In a position of utter desolation, when man cannot express himself in positive action, when his only achievement may consist in enduring his sufferings in the right way—an honorable way—in such a position man can, through loving contemplation of the image he carries of his beloved, achieve fulfillment.

VIKTOR FRANKL

Love is a gift of the universe. Like most of the bounty of the universe, it is distributed unevenly. It may come at the wrong time. It may arrive in what is clearly the wrong person. It may never come at all.

But when the right person and the right time coincide, we must be ready.

PHYLLIS HUBBELL

I Am the Song of Love

I am the song of love.
I murmur gently in the secret places.
When the lovers breathe the gladness of the sky;
When they laugh, and the cause of their mirth is hidden;
When they are awing with the bird, adrift with the cloud,
    astir with the leaves and the blades of grass and the
    spring:
I am the song they sing.

I am the purl of their caresses.
I am the cry of the passion of love.

I swell through the ardor of embracing;
Tongue whispers me to tongue, and I rise in the breast of the maiden;
I throb in the arms that encircle;
I beat in the legs that entwine;

I climb to a roar of ecstatic flow, man to woman,
The full-bellowed call of life.
Before the panting diminish, and the blissful anguish die,
I am the passion cry.

I am the rhythm of their silences.
I am the sob of the sorrow of love.
When the tigress haunts the jungle of her mind, solitary, baffled,
When her mate is caged in convention; is exhibited upon the
    highways of life;
I am the moan of her loneliness,
I am the howl of his rage.
When the stars glow unheeded above a lone, bowed head;
When longing lovers watch the studded air—each viewing
    other constellations;
When the low bell of midnight falls on the listening, unexpectant ear,
And the lark proclaims anew the impotent day;
When absence lays its hoar-frost on the soul;
When death has come to rob:
I am the sorrow-sob.

I am the eternal ever-changing song of love.

Joseph T. Shipley

We are not automatic lovers of self, others, world, or God. Love does not just happen. We are not love machines, puppets on the strings of a deity called "love." Love is a choice—not simply, or necessarily, a rational choice, but rather a willingness to be present to others without pretense or guile. Love is a conversion to humanity—a willingness to participate with others in the healing of a broken world and broken lives. Love is the choice to experience life as a member of the human family, a partner in the dance of life, rather than as an alien in the world or as a deity above the world, aloof and apart from human flesh.

Carter Heyward

Only love can bring individual beings to their perfect completion, as individuals, by uniting them one with another, because only love takes possession of them and unites them by what lies deepest within them. This is simply a fact of our everyday experience. For indeed at what moment do lovers come into the most complete possession of themselves if not when they say they are lost in one another? And is not love all the time achieving—in couples, in teams, all around us—the magical and reputedly contradictory feat of personalizing through totalizing? And why should not what is thus daily achieved on a small scale be repeated one day on world-wide dimensions?

Humanity, the spirit of the earth, the synthesis of individuals and peoples, the paradoxical conciliation of the element with the whole, of the one with the many: all these are regarded as utopian fantasies, yet they are biologically necessary; and if we would see them made flesh in the world what more need we do than imagine our power to love growing and broadening till it can embrace the totality of men and of the earth?

Pierre Teilhard de Chardin

We are neither animals nor angels. We are something else—we are humans—part spiritual and part physical, and those two parts are combined into one. A true sexuality acknowledges both these dimensions and tries to embrace them both in the act of love.

You need to accept this in yourself. Having sex is what the animals do. Achieving mystical union is what angels do. We alone can make love, where the physical and the spiritual commingle in a single, joyous act.

Kent Nerburn

Love is a high inducement for individuals to ripen, to strive to mature in the inner self, to manifest maturity in the outer world, to become that manifestation for the sake of another. This is a great, demanding task; it calls one to expand one's horizon greatly.

Rainer Maria Rilke

The freedom to marry is but a symbol of a far more important freedom, one that no law can successfully curtail. In the end our struggle is for the freedom to love. Love is divine, and no human power can contain it. A thousand years of tradition cannot deny it; a hundred laws cannot prevent it. In the end, love will always prevail.

DANIEL SCHATZ

The love of twos begins in miracle, and the miracle never wholly dies away even when the days of golden wedding near. A mystery like that of birth and that of death is the mystery of two young spirits all unconsciously through distant ways approaching, each fated at some turn, some instant, to find and recognize the other. Follows, then, the second and continuing mystery of the two becoming very one.

WILLIAM CHANNING GANNETT

Ah Love! could you and I with Him conspire
To grasp this sorry Scheme of Things entire,
Would not we shatter it to bits—and then
Remold it nearer to the Heart's desire!

EDWARD FITZGERALD

'Tis the gift to be simple
'Tis the gift to be free
'Tis the gift to come down
Where we ought to be

And when we find ourselves
In the place just right
It will be in the valley
Of love and delight.

SHAKER HYMN

Said Solomon to Sheba,
And kissed her Arab eyes,
"There's not a man or woman
Born under the skies
Dare match in learning with us two,
And all day long we have found
There's not a thing but love can make
The world a narrow pound."

WILLIAM BUTLER YEATS

Vision

To-day there have been lovely things
I never saw before;
Sunlight through a jar of marmalade;
A blue gate;
A rainbow
In soapsuds on dishwater;
Candlelight on butter;
The crinkled smile of a little girl
Who had new shoes with tassels;
A chickadee on a thorn-apple;
Empurpled mud under a willow,
Where white geese slept;
White ruffled curtains sifting moonlight
On the scrubbed kitchen floor;
The under side of a white-oak leaf;
Ruts in the road at sunset;
An egg yolk in a blue bowl.

My love kissed my eyes last night.

MAY THIELGAARD WATTS

Somewhere there waiteth in this world of ours
For one lone soul another lonely soul,
Each choosing each through all the weary hours,
And meeting strangely at one sudden goal,
Then blend they, like green leaves with golden flowers,
Into one beautiful and perfect whole;
And life's long night is ended, and the way
Lies open onward to eternal day.

EDWIN ARNOLD

Love is something eternal—the aspect may change, but not the essence. There is the same difference in a person before and after he is in love as there is in an unlighted candle and one that is burning. The candle was there and it was a good candle, but now it is shedding light, too, and that is its real function.

VINCENT VAN GOGH

I am he that aches with amorous love;
Does the earth gravitate? does not all matter, aching, attract all matter?
So the body of me to all I meet or know.

WALT WHITMAN

Love is an outgoing movement, an impulse toward another person, toward an existence separate and distinct from one's own, toward an end in view, a future.

SIMONE DE BEAUVOIR

These I have loved:
    White plates and cups, clean-gleaming,
Ringed with blue lines; and feathery, faery dust;
Wet roofs, beneath the lamp-light; the strong crust
Of friendly bread; and many-tasting food;
Rainbows; and the blue bitter smoke of wood;
And radiant raindrops couching in cool flowers;
And flowers themselves, that sway through sunny hours,
Dreaming of moths that drink them under the moon;
Then, the cool kindliness of sheets, that soon
Smooth away trouble; and the rough male kiss
Of blankets; grainy wood; live hair that is
Shining and free; blue-massing clouds; the keen
Unpassioned beauty of a great machine;
The benison of hot water; furs to touch;
The good smell of old clothes; and other such—
The comfortable smell of friendly fingers,
Hair's fragrance, and the musty reek that lingers
About dead leaves and last year's ferns. . . .

RUPERT BROOKE

If death be good,
Why do the gods not die?
If life be ill,
Why do the gods still live?

If love be naught,
Why do the gods still love?
If love be all,
What should men do but love?

BLISS CARMAN

Gifts

I gave my first love laughter,
    I gave my second tears,
I gave my third love silence
    Through all the years.

My first love gave me singing,
    My second eyes to see,
But oh, it was my third love
    Who gave my soul to me.

SARA TEASDALE

"Goodbye," said the fox. "And now here is my secret, a very simple secret: It is only with the heart that one can see rightly: what is essential is invisible to the eye."

"What is essential is invisible to the eye," the little prince repeated, so that he would be sure to remember.

ANTOINE DE SAINT-EXUPÉRY

No man ever forgot the visitations of that power to his heart and brain, which created all things anew; which was the dawn in him of music, poetry, and art; which made the face of nature radiant with purple light, the morning and the night varied enchantments; when a single tone of one voice could make the heart bound, and the most trivial circumstance associated with one form is put in the amber of memory; when he became all eye when one was present, and all memory when one was gone; when the youth becomes a watcher of windows and studious of a glove, a veil, a ribbon, or the wheels of a carriage; when no place is too solitary and none too silent, for him who has richer company and sweeter conversation in his new thoughts than any old friends, though best and purest, can give him; for the figures, the motions, the words of the beloved object are not like other images written in water, but, as Plutarch said, "enamelled in fire," and make the study of midnight.

RALPH WALDO EMERSON

You can transmute love, ignore it, muddle it, but you can never pull it out of you. I know by experience that the poets are right: love is eternal.

E. M. FORSTER

He who knows Love becomes Love, and he knows
    All beings are himself, twin-born of Love.
Melted in Love's own fire, his spirit flows
    Into all earthly forms, below, above;
He is the breath and glamour of the rose,
    He is the benediction of the dove.

ELSA BARKER

Love is enough: though the World be a-waning
And the woods have no voice but the voice of complaining,
    Though the sky be too dark for dim eyes to discover
The gold-cups and daisies fair blooming thereunder,
Though the hills be held shadows, and the sea a dark wonder,
    And this day draw a veil over all deeds passed over,
Yet their hands shall not tremble, their feet shall not falter;
The void shall not weary, the fear shall not alter
    These lips and these eyes of the loved and the lover.

WILLIAM MORRIS

If I truly love one person I love all persons, I love the world, I love life. If I can say to somebody else, "I love you," I must be able to say, "I love in you everybody, I love through you the world, I love in you also myself."

ERICH FROMM

Gadzooks! What a big chunk of God is to be found by looking into the face of someone you love!

LORNA LANDVIK

Love rules the court, the camp, the grove,
And men below and saints above;
For love is heaven, and heaven is love.

SIR WALTER SCOTT

We reach the divine through some one, and by dividing our joy with this one we double it, and come in touch with the universal. The sky is never so blue, the birds never sing so blithely, our acquaintances are never so gracious as when we are filled with love for some one.

ELBERT HUBBARD

Love

All thoughts, all passions, all delights,
Whatever stirs this mortal frame,
All are but ministers of Love,
    And feed his sacred flame.

SAMUEL TAYLOR COLERIDGE

To love is to find your own soul
Through the soul of the beloved one.

EDGAR LEE MASTERS

love is more thicker than forget
more thinner than recall
more seldom than a wave is wet
more frequent than to fail

it is most mad and moonly
and less it shall unbe
than all the sea which only
is deeper than the sea

love is less always than to win
less never than alive
less bigger than the least begin
less littler than forgive

it is more sane and sunly
and more it cannot die
than all the sky which only
is higher than the sky

E. E. CUMMINGS

A Birthday

My heart is like a singing bird
    Whose nest is in a watered shoot:
My heart is like an apple-tree
    Whose boughs are bent with thickset fruit;
My heart is like a rainbow shell
    That paddles in a halcyon sea;
My heart is gladder than all these
    Because my love is come to me.

Raise me a dais of silk and down;
    Hang it with vair and purple dyes;
Carve it in doves and pomegranates,
    And peacocks with a hundred eyes;
Work it in gold and silver grapes,
    In leaves and silver fleurs-de-lys;
Because the birthday of my life
    Is come, my love is come to me.

CHRISTINA ROSSETTI

So through the eyes love attains the heart:
For the eyes are the scouts of the heart,
And the eyes go reconnoitering
For what it would please the heart to possess.
And when they are in full accord
And firm, all three, in the one resolve,
At that time, perfect love is born
From what the eyes have made welcome to the heart.
Not otherwise can love either be born or have commencement
Than by this birth and commencement moved by inclination.

By the grace and by command
Of these three, and from their pleasure,
Love is born, who its fair hope
Goes comforting her friends.
For as all true lovers
Know, love is perfect kindness,
Which is born—there is no doubt—from the heart and eyes.
The eyes make it blossom; the heart matures it:
Love, which is the fruit of their very seed.

GUIRAUT DE BORNEILH

Stone walls do not a prison make,
  Nor iron bars a cage;
Minds innocent and quiet take
  That for an hermitage;
If I have freedom in my love
  And in my soul am free,
Angels alone, that soar above,
  Enjoy such liberty.

RICHARD LOVELACE

We Are, Therefore, We Love

We are, therefore, we love.
Cosmic bits of mass and energy
Come to life together.
We love, therefore, we are.
May we be humbled before the wonder
Of what we dare to create.

RICHARD S. GILBERT

A Love Song

My love it should be silent, being deep—
And being very peaceful should be still—
Still as the utmost depths of ocean keep—
Serenely silent as some mighty hill.

Yet is my love so great it needs must fill
With very joy the inmost heart of me,
The joy of dancing branches on the hill
The joy of leaping waves upon the sea.

THEODOSIA GARRISON

If there is anything that may properly be called happiness here below, I am persuaded it is the union of two persons who love each other with perfect liberty, who are united by a secret inclination, and satisfied with each other's merits. Their hearts are full and leave no vacancy for any other passion; they enjoy perpetual tranquillity because they enjoy content.

HÉLOISE

Husbands should love their wives as they do their own bodies. He who loves his wife loves himself. For no one ever hates his own body, but he nourishes and tenderly cares for it, just as Christ does for the church, because we are members of his body. For this reason a man will leave his father and mother and be joined to his wife, and the two shall become one flesh.

EPHESIANS 5:28-31

Nothing in life is as good as the marriage of true minds between man and woman. As good? It is life itself.

PEARL S. BUCK

Who knows of the possibilities of love when men and women share not only children, home, and garden, not only the fulfillment of their biological roles, but the responsibilities and passions of the work that creates the human future and the full human knowledge of who they are?

BETTY FRIEDAN

Love. What a small word we use for an idea so immense and powerful it has altered the flow of history, calmed monsters, kindled works of art, cheered the forlorn, turned tough guys to mush, consoled the enslaved, driven strong women mad, glorified the humble, fueled national scandals, bankrupted robber barons, and made mincemeat of kings. How can love's spaciousness be conveyed in the narrow confines of one syllable?

DIANE ACKERMAN

Give all to love;
Obey thy heart;
Friends, kindred, days,
Estate, good fame,
Plans, credit, and the muse;
Nothing refuse.

'Tis a brave master,
Let it have scope,
Follow it utterly,
Hope beyond hope;
High and more high,
It dives into noon,
With wing unspent,
Untold intent;

But 'tis a god,
Knows its own path,
And the outlets of the sky.
'Tis not for the mean,
It requireth courage stout,
Souls above doubt,
Valor unbending;
Such 'twill reward,
They shall return
More than they were,
And ever ascending.

RALPH WALDO EMERSON

If I speak in the tongues of mortals and of angels, but do not have love, I am a noisy gong or a clanging cymbal. And if I have prophetic powers, and understand all mysteries and all knowledge, and if I have all faith, so as to remove mountains, but do not have love, I am nothing. If I give away all my possessions, and if I hand over my body so that I may boast, but do not have love, I gain nothing.

Love is patient; love is kind; love is not envious or boastful or arrogant or rude. It does not insist on its own way; it is not irritable or resentful; it does not rejoice in wrongdoing, but rejoices in the truth. It bears all things, believes all things, hopes all things, endures all things.

1 CORINTHIANS 13

Blessings We Would Pray

Prayer

Lord, now Thy rich, rare blessings we would pray
On these who pledge their love and gladly go
Toward destiny—be it of joy or woe
And may their memory ever find its way
Back to the tender impulse of this day:
And may affection's ties abound and grow
As each unselfish sharing makes it so:
From our hearts' depths these blessings now we pray.

ROSCOE E. TRUEBLOOD

It is one of life's richest surprises when the accidental meeting of two life paths leads them to proceed together along the common path of man and wife, and it is one of life's finest experiences when a casual relationship grows into a permanent bond of love. This meeting and this growth bring us together today.

ANONYMOUS

Epithalamium

I saw two clouds at morning,
    Tinged with the rising sun,
And in the dawn they floated on,
    And mingled into one:
I thought that morning cloud was blest,
It moved so sweetly to the west.

I saw two summer currents
    Flow smoothly to their meeting,
And join their course, with silent force,
    In peace each other greeting:
Calm was their course through banks of green,
While dimpling eddies played between.

Such be your gentle motion,
    Till life's last pulse shall beat;
Like summer's beam, and summer's stream,
    Float on, in joy, to meet
A calmer sea, where storms shall cease—
A purer sky, where all is peace.

JOHN GARDINER CALKINS BRAINARD

Hear the mellow wedding bells—
Golden bells!
What a world of happiness their harmony foretells!
Through the balmy air of night
How they ring out their delight!—
From the molten-golden notes,
What a liquid ditty floats
To the turtle-dove that listens, while she gloats
On the moon!
Oh, from out the sounding cells,
What a gush of euphony voluminously wells!
How it swells!
How it dwells
On the Future!—how it tells
Of the rapture that impels
To the swinging and the ringing
Of the bells, bells, bells—
Of the bells, bells, bells, bells,
Bells, bells, bells—
To the rhyming and the chiming of the bells!

EDGAR ALLAN POE

At the Wedding March

God with honour hang your head,
Groom, and grace you, bride, your bed
With lissome scions, sweet scions,
Out of hallowed bodies bred.

Each be other's comfort kind:
Deep, deeper than divined,
Divine charity, dear charity,
Fast you ever, fast bind.

Then let the March tread our ears:
I to him turn with tears
Who to wedlock, his wonder wedlock,
Deals triumph and immortal years.

GERARD MANLEY HOPKINS

Let the love of this hour go on; let all the oaths and children and people
of this love be clean as a washed stone under a waterfall in the sun.

CARL SANDBURG

Sanctification

Ceremony of sapphire skies
and emerald grasses
with an altar of marble
and open doors

Ceremony of everywhere
near and far

We stand by fountains of flowers
and pews of pine
We congregate with many

Around us we hear
hymns of the earth
songs universal

A golden chalice of fire
illuminates our vows the genesis
of "our promising new life"
we unite together
side by side.

CAROLYN SIBR

We meet on holy ground,
Brought into being as life encounters life,
As personal histories merge into the communal story,
As we take on the pride and pain of our companions,
As separate selves become community.

How desperate is our need for one another:
Our silent beckoning to our neighbors,
Our invitations to share life and death together,
Our welcome into the lives of those we meet,
And their welcome into our own.

May our souls capture this treasured time.
May our spirits celebrate our meeting
In this time and in this space,
For we meet on holy ground.

RICHARD S. GILBERT

If the couple believes there's magic in the ceremony, then there is. If they believe they have a very special relationship, then they do. If they say before their friends and relatives that their relationship is very special, then it is. If they say it in a church or a sacred grove or a meadow with a robed person, then perhaps they believe it even more. I don't "pronounce" them man and wife. I say "you have made a marriage, and we here are glad to recognize it." The state doesn't make a marriage. A marriage happens between two people, and the state simply recognizes that it exists.

WEBSTER KITCHELL

Look to this day!
For it is life, the very life of life.
In its brief course lie all the verities
and realities of your existence:
   The bliss of growth,
   The glory of action,
   The splendor of beauty;
For yesterday is but a dream,
And tomorrow is only a vision;
But today, well lived, makes every yesterday
A dream of happiness
And every tomorrow a vision of hope.
Look well, therefore, to this day.

KALIDASA

Happily the old men will regard you.
Happily the old women will regard you.
Happily the young men will regard you.
Happily the young women will regard you.
Happily the boys will regard you.
Happily the girls will regard you.
Happily the children will regard you.
Happily the chiefs will regard you.
Happily, as they scatter in different directions, they will regard you.
Happily, as they approach their homes, they will regard you.
Happily may their roads home be on the trail of pollen.
Happily may they all get back.
In beauty I walk.
With beauty before me, I walk.
With beauty behind me, I walk.
With beauty below me, I walk.
With beauty above me, I walk.
With beauty all around me, I walk.
It is finished in beauty.
It is finished in beauty.
It is finished in beauty.
It is finished in beauty.

NAVAJO NIGHT CHANT

When you say to one another, "I love you,"
be able to say, "I love in you everyone.
I love through you the world.
I love life.
I love in you also myself."
In loving one another, you make it possible to love more.
As you hold each other,
know you are held in a larger embrace.
We are all connected
and your choice of commitment affects us all.
Your commitment strengthens our fidelity to one another,
for we depend on one another more than we know.
May your love for one another enlarge your embrace—
to love people,
the earth,
life,
and yourselves.
So much is possible.
May love, wherever it is found, be celebrated and recognized.
We see the love between you
and we know your days together will be good,
for you and for us all.
To be worthy of a gift, say so,
I do, yes, I do.
I promise with my heart, yes,
and with my mind, yes,

and with my body, yes,
for better, for worse,
for richer, for poorer,
in sickness and in health,
yes,
to love you always,
yes, oh yes.
To be worthy of this gift,
say so
and rejoice,
rejoice, rejoice.

BARBARA HAMILTON-HOLWAY

A Drinking Song

Wine comes in at the mouth
And love comes in at the eye;
That's all we know for truth
Before we grow old and die.
I lift the glass to my mouth,
I look at you, and I sigh.

WILLIAM BUTLER YEATS

Joy

Let a joy keep you.
Reach out your hands
And take it when it runs by,
As the Apache dancer
Clutches his woman.
I have seen them
Live long and laugh loud,
Sent on singing, singing,
Smashed to the heart
Under the ribs
With a terrible love.
Joy always,
Joy everywhere—
Let joy kill you!
Keep away from the little deaths.

CARL SANDBURG

We pray for concord and creativity as well as for love and laughter in their life together; and when there is pain, may there be peace that passes not away. We pray for joy that they will share with other people, and for their home; may it be a temple for that which is beautiful and good and true. As they share the richer experiences of life, so may their hearts and minds and souls be knit ever more closely together. And yet may their bonds of sympathy strengthen their separate personalities. We pray for courage for them when the road is rough, and for humility for them when fortune favors them. May they carry the past gratefully with them in all the years of their sojourn, and with an equal measure of hope ever face the future unafraid.

DANA MCLEAN GREELEY

In the quiet of this very special moment we pause to give thanks for all the rich experiences of life that have brought this couple to this high point in their lives. We are especially grateful for the values which have flowed into them from those who have loved them and nurtured them and pointed them along life's way. We are grateful that within them is the dream of a great love and the resources to use that love in creating a home that shall endure. We are grateful for the values which they have found by their own strivings.

And now as they make their promises to each other, may they make them with the deepest insight into their meaning and with their fullest sincerity. May this be but the beginning of a relationship that will grow and mature with each passing year until the latter days become even more wonderful than the first.

ROBERT BOTLEY

Always there is a beginning—
    a new day,
    a new month,
    a new season,
    a new year.

Forever the old passes away
    and newness emerges
    from the richness that was.
Nothing is ever lost
    in the many changes
    time brings.

What was, in some way,
    will be,
    though changed in form.

Know this:
This moment is a beginning;
And your lives,
    individually and together,
    are full of richness, of freshness,
    of hope and of promise.

EDWARD SEARL

Now you will feel no rain,
for each of you will be a shelter to the other.

Now you will feel no cold,
for each of you will be warmth to the other.

Now there is no loneliness for you;
Now there is no more loneliness.

Now you are two bodies,
but there is only one life before you.

Go now to your dwelling place,
to enter into your days together.

And may your days be good
and long on the earth.

Apache Song

blessing the boats

(at st. mary's)

may the tide
that is entering even now
the lip of our understanding
carry you out
beyond the face of fear
may you kiss
the wind then turn from it
certain that it will
love your back
may you
open your eyes to water
water waving forever
and may you in your innocence
sail through this to that

LUCILLE CLIFTON

Go now in peace.
Deeply regard each other;
Truly listen to each other;
Speak what each must speak;
Be ready to disarm your own heart;
Rejoice in this love you have begun.
Amen.

BARBARA HAMILTON-HOLWAY

I Would Follow Your Soul

I would live in your love as the sea-grasses live in the sea,
Borne up by each wave as it passes, drawn down by each wave that
    recedes;
I would empty my soul of the dreams that have gathered in me,
I would beat with your heart as it beats, I would follow your soul as it
    leads.

SARA TEASDALE

How do I love thee? Let me count the ways.
I love thee to the depth and breadth and height
My soul can reach, when feeling out of sight
For the ends of Being and ideal Grace.
I love thee to the level of everyday's
Most quiet need, by sun and candle-light.
I love thee freely, as men strive for Right;
I love thee purely, as they turn from Praise.
I love thee with the passion put to use
In my old griefs, and with my childhood's faith.
I love thee with a love I seemed to lose
With my lost saints,—I love thee with the breath,
Smiles, tears, of all my life!—and, if God choose,
I shall but love thee better after death.

ELIZABETH BARRETT BROWNING

Song of Psyyha

I love you passionately!
I love you as I love the sun overhead,
The earth underfoot,
The flowers that spring out of the earth,
The fresh breezes of the sea,
The morning star, gold-fluctuating Venus,
Or calm white steadfast Jupiter.

I love you passionately!
The brawny beautiful arms made for enfolding,
The eyes brown and limpid, brimming over with sweetness.

It is necessary to me that your heart beats,
And that you inhale with conscious pleasure the soft spring air,
That you love light, color, action, and are ambitious,
That you love the beauty of the human face and form,
And portray them both with mastery;
That you grasp that which is not graspable by all,
And know that which is not knowable to all;
That you have eyes—for a purpose,
A heart—for a purpose,
And an inquisitive soul—for a purpose.

CHARLOTTE EATON

Doubt thou the stars are fire,
　　Doubt that the sun doth move,
Doubt truth to be a liar,
　　But never doubt I love.

WILLIAM SHAKESPEARE

(Hark close, and still, what I now whisper to you,
I love you—O you entirely possess me,
O I wish that you and I escape from the rest, and go utterly off—
　　O free and lawless,
Two hawks in the air—two fishes swimming in the sea not more
　　lawless than we;)
—The furious storm through me careening—I passionately trembling;

The oath of the inseparableness of two together—of the woman that
　　loves me, and whom
I love more than my life—that oath swearing;
(O I willingly stake all, for you!
O let me be lost, if it must be so!
O you and I—what is it to us what the rest do or think?
What is all else to us? only that we enjoy each other, and exhaust each
　　other, if it must be so:)

WALT WHITMAN

Pussy said to the Owl, "You elegant fowl,
How charmingly sweet you sing!
Oh! let us be married; too long we have tarried:
But what shall we do for a ring?"
They sailed away, for a year and a day,
To the land where the bong-tree grows;
And there in a wood a Piggy-wig stood,
With a ring at the end of his nose,
His nose,
His nose,
With a ring at the end of his nose.

"Dear Pig, are you willing to sell for one shilling
Your ring?" Said the Piggy, "I will."
So they took it away, and were married next day
By the Turkey who lives on the hill.
They dined on mince and slices of quince,
Which they ate with a runcible spoon;
And hand in hand, on the edge of the sand,
They danced by the light of the moon,
The moon,
The moon,
They danced by the light of the moon.

EDWARD LEAR

Dearest,—I wish I had the gift of making rhymes, for methinks there is poetry in my head and heart since I have been in love with you. You are a Poem. Of what sort, then? Epic? Mercy on me, no! A sonnet? No; for that is too labored and artificial. You are a sort of sweet, simple, gay, pathetic ballad, which Nature is singing, sometimes with tears, sometimes with smiles, and sometimes with intermingled smiles and tears.

NATHANIEL HAWTHORNE

Poet to His Love

An old silver church in a forest
Is my love for you.
The trees around it
Are words that I have stolen from your heart.
An old silver bell, the last smile you gave,
Hangs at the top of my church.
It rings only when you come through the forest
And stand beside it.
And then, it has no need for ringing,
For your voice takes its place.

MAXWELL BODENHEIM

I want to be your friend
For ever and ever without break or decay.
When the hills are all flat
And the rivers are all dry,
When it lightens and thunders in winter,
When it rains and snows in summer,
When heaven and earth mingle—
Not till then will I part from you.

CHINESE OATH

My deepest, strongest desire in marrying you, darling, is to make you happy, and I would put into this letter some word of love which would seem to your heart a sort of sweet preface to the book of love which we are about to open together, to read new secrets of sympathy and companionship. I would have you catch a glimpse of my purpose for the future and of the joy which that future contains for me, of the gratitude I feel for your priceless gift of love, and of the infinite love and tenderness which is the gift of my heart to you.

WOODROW WILSON

Love Song

I love my life, but not too well
    To give it to thee like a flower,
So it may pleasure thee to dwell
    Deep in its perfume but an hour.
I love my life, but not too well.

I love my life, but not too well
    To sing it note by note away,
So to thy soul the song may tell
    The beauty of the desolate day.
I love my life, but not too well.

I love my life but not too well
    To cast it like a cloak on thine,
Against the storms that sound and swell
    Between thy lonely heart and mine.
I love my life, but not too well.

HARRIET MONROE

I married a rich woman—one rich in love, loyalty, gentleness, insight, gratitude, appreciation. One who caused me, at thirty-three years of age, to be born again.

To this woman I owe all I am—and to her the world owes its gratitude for any and all, be it much or little, that I have given it. My religion is all in my wife's name. And I am not bankrupt, for all she has is mine, if I can use it, and in degree I have.

And why I prize life, and desire to live, is that I may give the world more of the treasures of her heart and mind, realizing with perfect faith, that the supply coming from Infinity, can never be lessened nor decreased.

ELBERT HUBBARD

You are my wife
My feet shall run because of you.
My feet, dance because of you.
My heart shall beat because of you.
My eyes, see because of you.
My mind, think because of you.
And I shall love because of you.

ESKIMO LOVE SONG

Poem in Prose

This poem is for my wife.
I have made it plainly and honestly:
The mark is on it
Like the burl on the knife.

I have not made it for praise.
She has no more need for praise
Than summer has
Or the bright days.

In all that becomes a woman
Her words and her ways are beautiful:
Love's lovely duty,
The well-swept room.

Wherever she is there is sun
And time and a sweet air:
Peace is there,
Work done.

There are always curtains and flowers
And candles and baked bread
And a cloth spread
And a clean house.

Her voice when she sings is a voice
At dawn by a freshening sea
Where the wave leaps in the
Wind and rejoices.

Wherever she is it is now.
It is here where the apples are:
Here in the stars,
In the quick hour.

The greatest and richest good,
My own life to live in,
This she has given me—

If giver could.

ARCHIBALD MacLEISH

I love you as certain dark things are loved,
secretly, between the shadow and the soul.

PABLO NERUDA

To My Dear and Loving Husband

If ever two were one then surely we.
If ever man were loved by wife, then thee;
If ever wife was happy in a man,
Compare with me, ye women, if you can.
I prize thy love more than whole mines of gold
Or all the riches that the East doth hold.
My love is such that rivers cannot quench,
Nor aught but love from thee give recompense.
Thy love is such I can no way repay,
The heavens reward thee manifold, I pray.
Then while we live, in love let's so persevere
That when we live no more, we may live ever.

ANNE BRADSTREET

If all else perished, and *he* remained, I should still continue to be;
and, if all else remained, and he were annihilated, the Universe would
turn to a mighty stranger. I should not seem a part of it.

EMILY BRONTË

Opal

You are ice and fire,
The touch of you burns my hands like snow.
You are cold and flame.
You are the crimson of amaryllis,
The silver of moon-touched magnolias.
When I am with you,
My heart is a frozen pond
Gleaming with agitated torches.

AMY LOWELL

Faults

They came to tell your faults to me,
They named them over one by one;
I laughed aloud when they were done,
I knew them all so well before,—
Oh, they were blind, too blind to see
Your faults had made me love you more.

SARA TEASDALE

Wild nights! Wild nights!
Were I with thee,
Wild nights should be
Our luxury!

Futile the winds
To a heart in port,—
Done with the compass,
Done with the chart.

Rowing in Eden!
Ah! the sea!
Might I but moor
To-night in thee!

EMILY DICKINSON

I hereby give myself. I love you. You are the only being whom I can love absolutely with my complete self, with all my flesh and mind and heart. You are my mate, my perfect partner, and I am yours.

IRIS MURDOCH

Where We Belong, A Duet

In every town and village,
In every city square,
In crowded places
I searched the faces
Hoping to find
Someone to care.

I read mysterious meanings
In the distant stars,
Then I went to schoolrooms
And poolrooms
And half-lighted cocktail bars.
Braving dangers,
Going with strangers,
I don't even remember their names.
I was quick and breezy
And always easy
Playing romantic games.

I wined and dined a thousand exotic Joans and Janes
In dusty dance halls, at debutante balls,
On lonely country lanes.
I fell in love forever,
Twice every year or so.
I wooed them sweetly, was theirs completely,

But they always let me go.
Saying bye now, no need to try now,
You don't have the proper charms.
Too sentimental and much too gentle
I don't tremble in your arms.

Then you rose into my life
Like a promised sunrise.
Brightening my days with the light in your eyes.
I've never been so strong,
Now I'm where I belong.

Maya Angelou

Your words are my food, your breath my wine—you are everything
to me.

Sarah Bernhardt

The Sun Has Burst the Sky

The sun has burst the sky
Because I love you
And the river its banks.

The sea laps the great rocks
Because I love you
And takes no heed of the moon dragging it away
And saying coldly "Constancy is not for you."

The blackbird fills the air
Because I love you
With spring and lawns and shadows falling on lawns.

The people walk in the street and laugh
I love you
And far down the river ships sound their hooters
Crazy with joy because I love you.

JENNY JOSEPH

A Red, Red Rose

O my Luve's like a red, red rose,
    That's newly sprung in June:
O my Luve's like the melodie,
    That's sweetly play'd in tune.

As fair art thou, my bonnie lass,
    So deep in luve am I;
And I will luve thee still, my dear,
    Till a' the seas gang dry.

Till a' the seas gang dry, my dear,
    And the rocks melt wi' the sun;
And I will luve thee still, my dear,
    While the sands o' life shall run.

And fare-thee-weel, my only Luve!
    And fare-thee-weel, a while!
And I will come again, my Luve,
    Tho' 'twere ten thousand mile!

ROBERT BURNS

The First Day

I wish I could remember the first day,
First hour, first moment of your meeting me;
If bright or dim the season, it might be
Summer or winter for aught I can say.
So unrecorded did it slip away,
So blind was I to see and to foresee,
So dull to mark the budding of my tree
That would not blossom yet for many a May.
If only I could recollect it! Such
A day of days! I let it come and go
As traceless as a thaw of bygone snow.
It seemed to mean so little, meant so much!
If only now I could recall that touch,
First touch of hand in hand!—Did one but know!

CHRISTINA ROSSETTI

She had filled me with some previously unimaginable power which
I knew I could and would use in my art. The deep causes of the uni-
verse, the stars, and the galaxies, the ultimate particles of matter, had
fashioned these two things, my love and my art, as aspects of what
was ultimately one and the same.

IRIS MURDOCH

Like a quetzal plume, a fragrant flower,
friendship sparkles
Like heron plums, it weaves itself into finery.
Our song is a bird calling out like a jingle
how beautiful you make it sound!
Here, among flowers that enclose us,
Among flowery boughs you are singing.

AZTEC POEM

When I told Alma the things I saw she would laugh and tell me she loved my imagination. For her I changed pebbles into diamonds, shoes into mirrors, I changed glass into water, I gave her wings and pulled birds from her ears and in her pockets she found the feathers, I asked a pear to become a pineapple, a pineapple to become a lightbulb, a lightbulb to become the moon, and the moon to become a coin I flipped for her love, both sides were heads: I knew I couldn't lose.

NICOLE KRAUSS

George and Helen arose and walked away into the darkness. They went along a path past a field of corn that had not yet been cut. The wind whispered among the dry corn blades. For a moment during the walk back into town the spell that held them was broken. When they had come to the crest of Waterworks Hill they stopped by a tree and George again put his hands on the girl's shoulders. She embraced him eagerly and then again they drew quickly back from that impulse. They stopped kissing and stood a little apart. Mutual respect grew big in them. They were both embarrassed and to relieve their embarrassment dropped into the animalism of youth. They laughed and began to pull and haul at each other. In some way chastened and purified by the mood they had been in, they became, not man and woman, not boy and girl, but excited little animals.

It was so they went down the hill. In the darkness they played like two splendid young things in a young world. Once, running swiftly forward, Helen tripped George and he fell. He squirmed and shouted. Shaking with laughter, he rolled down the hill. Helen ran after him. For just a moment she stopped in the darkness. There was no way of knowing what woman's thoughts went through her mind but, when the bottom of the hill was reached and she came up to the boy, she took his arm and walked beside him in dignified silence. For some reason they could not have explained they had both got from their silent evening together the thing needed. Man or boy, woman or girl, they had for a moment taken hold of the thing that makes the mature life of men and women in the modern world possible.

SHERWOOD ANDERSON

The Lover Sings of a Garden

Oh, beautiful are the flowers of your garden,
 The flowers of your garden are fair:
Blue flowers of your eyes
 And dusk flower of your hair;
Dew flower of your mouth
 And peony-budded breasts,
And the flower of the curve of your hand
 Where my hand rests.

HELEN HOYT

Oh,
I am thinking
Oh,
I am thinking
I have found
my lover.
Oh,
I think it is so.

CHIPPEWA SONG

67

To Celia

Drink to me only with thine eyes,
 And I will pledge with mine;
Or leave a kiss but in the cup
 And I'll not look for wine.
The thirst that from the soul doth rise
 Doth ask a drink divine;
But might I of Jove's nectar sup,
 I would not change for thine.

I sent thee late a rosy wreath,
 Not so much honouring thee
As giving it a hope that there
 It could not wither'd be;
But thou thereon didst only breathe,
 And sent'st it back to me;
Since when it grows, and smells, I swear,
 Not of itself but thee!

BEN JOHNSON

A Love Poem

For this and that;
these and those.

For from and to;
then and when.

For how and why;
near and far.

But most of all
for you and me—
here and now.

EDWARD SEARL

Words Are Just Words

Have I told you your smile
It comes without warning
Brings pictures of kitchen
Of honey and morning,
Of sunshine
And yellow canary birds sing
But words are just words

Your smile
Now that's the real thing!

And the sound of your laughter
When we're running together
It's like wind in the shingles
And October weather.
Like pushing the children
Up high on a swing
Your laughter however
That's the real thing!

Have I told you I love you
Well how could I say it
With couplets
And verses
I'd never convey it.
Words may be pretty
As beads on a string
But words
Are just words

Would you settle
For the real thing?

RIC MASTEN

I Love Thee

I love thee—I love thee!
      'Tis all that I can say;—
It is my vision in the night,
      My dreaming in the day;
The very echo of my heart,
      The blessing when I pray:
I love thee—I love thee!
      Is all that I can say.

I love thee—I love thee!
      Is ever on my tongue;
In all my proudest poesy
      That chorus still is sung;
It is the verdict of my eyes,
      Amidst the gay and young:
I love thee—I love thee!
      A thousand maids among.

I love thee—I love thee!
      Thy bright hazel glance,
The mellow lute upon those lips,
      Whose tender tones entrance;

But most, dear heart of hearts, thy proofs
    That still these words enhance,
I love thee—I love thee!
    Whatever be thy chance.

THOMAS HOOD

She Walks in Beauty

She walks in beauty, like the night
    Of cloudless climes and starry skies;
And all that's best of dark and bright
    Meet in her aspect and her eyes:
Thus mellow'd to that tender light
    Which heaven to gaudy day denies.
One shade the more, one ray the less,
    Had half impair'd the nameless grace
Which waves in every raven tress,
    Or softly lightens o'er her face;
Where thoughts serenely sweet express
    How pure, how dear their dwelling-place.

And on that cheek, and o'er that brow,
    So soft, so calm, yet eloquent,
The smiles that win, the tints that glow,
    But tell of days in goodness spent,

A mind at peace with all below,
  A heart whose love is innocent!

GEORGE GORDON LORD BYRON

My bounty is as boundless as the sea,
My love as deep; the more I give to thee,
The more I have, for both are infinite.

WILLIAM SHAKESPEARE

A White Rose

The red rose whispers of passion,
  And the white rose breathes of love;
O the red rose is a falcon,
  And the white rose is a dove.

But I send you a cream-white rosebud
  With a flush on its petal tips;
For the love that is purest and sweetest
  Has a kiss of desire on the lips.

JOHN BOYLE O'REILLY

Rondel of Merciless Beauty

Your two great eyes will slay me suddenly;
Their beauty shakes me who was once serene;
Straight through my heart the wound is quick and keen.

Only your word will heal the injury
To my hurt heart, while yet the wound is clean—
Your two great eyes will slay me suddenly;
Their beauty shakes me who was once serene.

Upon my word, I tell you faithfully
Through life and after death you are my queen;
For with my death the whole truth shall be seen.
Your two great eyes will slay me suddenly;
Their beauty shakes me who was once serene;
Straight through my heart the wound is quick and keen.

GEOFFREY CHAUCER

What does not perish
Lives in thee.

KENNETH PATCHEN

Sonnet 18

Shall I compare thee to a summer's day?
Thou art more lovely and more temperate:
Rough winds do shake the darling buds of May,
And summer's lease hath all too short a date:
Sometime too hot the eye of heaven shines,
And often is his gold complexion dimm'd;
And every fair from fair sometime declines,
By chance or nature's changing course untrimm'd;
But thy eternal summer shall not fade
Nor lose possession of that fair thou owest;
Nor shall Death brag thou wander'st in his shade,
When in eternal lines to time thou growest:
So long as men can breathe or eyes can see,
So long lives this and this gives life to thee.

WILLIAM SHAKESPEARE

My Delight and Thy Delight

My delight and thy delight
Walking, like two angels white,
In the gardens of the night:

My desire and thy desire
Twining to a tongue of fire,
Leaping live, and laughing higher:

Thro' the everlasting strife
In the mystery of life.

Love, from whom the world begun,
Hath the secret of the sun.

Love can tell, and love alone,
Whence the million stars were strewn,
Why each atom knows its own,
How, in spite of woe and death,
Gay is life, and sweet is breath:

This he taught us, this we knew,
Happy in his science true,
Hand in hand as we stood
'Neath the shadows of the wood,
Heart to heart as we lay
In the dawning of the day.

ROBERT BRIDGES

Love's Springtide

My heart was winter-bound until
    I heard you sing;
O voice of Love, hush not, but fill
    My life with Spring!

My hopes were homeless things before
    I saw your eyes;
O smile of Love, close not the door
    To paradise!

My dreams were bitter once, and then
    I found them bliss;
O lips of Love, give me again
    Your rose to kiss!

Springtide of Love! The secret sweet
    Is ours alone;
O heart of Love, at last you beat
    Against my own!

FRANK DEMPSTER SHERMAN

The Good Morrow

    I wonder by my troth, what thou and I
        Did, till we loved? were we not weaned till then?
    But sucked on country pleasures, childishly?
        Or snorted we i'the seven sleepers' den?
    'Twas so; But this, all pleasures fancies be.
    If ever any beauty I did see,
Which I desired, and got, 'twas but a dream of thee.

    And now good morrow to our waking souls,
        Which watch not one another out of fear;
    For love, all love of other sights controls,
        And makes one little room, an everywhere.
    Let sea-discoverers to new worlds have gone,
    Let maps to others, worlds on worlds have shown,
Let us possess our world, each hath one, and is one.

    My face in thine eye, thine in mine appears,
        And true plain hearts do in the faces rest,
    Where can we find two better hemispheres
        Without sharp North, without declining West?
    Whatever dies, was not mixed equally;
    If our two loves be one, or, thou and I
Love so alike, that none do slacken, none can die.

JOHN DONNE

I love thee, as I love the calm
    Of sweet, star-lighted hours!
I love thee, as I love the balm
    Of early jes'mine flow'rs.

I love thee, as I love the last
    Rich smile of fading day,
Which lingereth, like the look we cast,
    On rapture pass'd away.

I love thee as I love the tone
    Of some soft-breathing flute
Whose soul is wak'd for me alone,
    When all beside is mute.

I love thee as I love the first
    Young violent of the spring;
Or the pale lily, April-nurs'd,
    To scented blossoming.

I love thee, as I love the full,
    Clear gushings of the song,
Which lonely—sad—and beautiful—
    At night-fall floats along,

Pour'd by the bul-bul forth to greet
   The hours of rest and dew;
When melody and moonlight meet
   To blend their charm, and hue.

I love thee, as the glad bird loves
   The freedom of its wing,
On which delightedly it moves
   In wildest wandering.

I love thee as I love the swell
   And hush, of some low strain,
Which bringeth, by its gentle spell,
   The past to life again.

Such is the feeling which from thee
   Nought earthly can allure:
'Tis ever link'd to all I see
   Of gifted—high—and pure!

ELIZA ACTON

The Words We Say

In love there is a logic of gestures
    we don't interpret but trust,
        a courtship outlasting
    our beauty and our grief:

your face at rest above a book,
    your hand rising across the yard,
        suggesting a hedge, a summerhouse,
    or dropping flat-palmed to your chest.

A turning away in sleep,
    a turning back—
        we learn from it for years:
    approach one another,

wave like infants as we meet,
    or throw off the embrace,
        afraid to be tested, afraid
    as if we could do more than this,

give more than this
    (the body's full tilt,
        undisguised and honorable
    and the full light of attention)

as if to press our skulls
    against each other's,
        waterbirds eye to eye,
    were not enough,

as if we could make love
    transform us—
        never fall away, separate
    as the words we say and mean.

JODY BOLZ

two mouths
one ripe fig
so sweet . . .

JOSEPH KIRSCHNER

Topography

After we flew across the country we
got into bed, laid our bodies
delicately together, like maps laid
face to face, East to West, my
San Francisco against your New York, your
Fire Island against my Sonoma, my
New Orleans deep in your Texas, your Idaho
bright on my Great Lakes, my Kansas
burning against your Kansas your Kansas
burning against my Kansas, your Eastern
Standard Time pressing into my
Pacific Time, my Mountain Time
beating against your Central Time, your
sun rising swiftly from the right my
sun rising swiftly from the left your
moon rising slowly from the left my
moon rising slowly from the right until
all four bodies of the sky
burn above us, sealing us together,
all our cities twin cities,
all our states united, one
nation, indivisible, with liberty and justice for all.

SHARON OLDS

The Ache of It

The Ache of Marriage

The ache of marriage:

thigh and tongue, beloved,
are heavy with it,
it throbs in the teeth

We look for communion
and are turned away, beloved,
each and each

It is leviathan and we
in its belly
looking for joy, some joy
not to be known outside it

two by two in the ark of
the ache of it.

DENISE LEVERTOV

For one human being to love another is perhaps the most difficult
task of all, the epitome, the ultimate test. It is that striving for which
all other striving is merely preparation.

RAINER MARIA RILKE

Marriage is a rooted thing, a growing and flowering thing that must be tended faithfully.

Donald Culross Peattie

When you love someone you do not love them all the time, in exactly the same way, from moment to moment. It is an impossibility. It is even a lie to pretend to. And yet this is exactly what most of us demand. We have so little faith in the ebb and flow of life, of love, of relationships. We leap at the flow of the tide and resist in terror its ebb. We are afraid it will never return. We insist on permanency, on duration, on continuity; when the only continuity possible, in life as in love, is in growth, in fluidity—in freedom, in the sense that the dancers are free, barely touching as they pass, but partners in the same pattern. The only real security is not in owning or possessing, not in demanding or expecting, not in hoping, even. Security in a relationship lies neither in looking back to what it was in nostalgia, nor forward to what it might be in dread or anticipation, but living in the present relationship and accepting it as it is now. For relationships, too, must be like islands. One must accept them for what they are here and now, within their limits—islands, surrounded and interrupted by the sea, continually visited and abandoned by the tides. One must accept the security of the wingèd life, of ebb and flow, of intermittency.

Anne Morrow Lindbergh

Perhaps every long marriage follows these five stages: 1. Darling, you are perfect. 2. Good grief! You seem to have a few foibles. 3. Let me help you get rid of your foibles so you will indeed be perfect. 4. Okay, I love you in spite of your foibles. 5. I can't believe this has happened. I sometimes love you because of your foibles.

BARBARA ROHDE

Old-fashioned Requited Love

I have ransacked the encyclopedias
And slid my fingers among topics and titles
Looking for you.

And the answer comes slow.
There seems to be no answer.

I shall ask the next banana peddler the who and the why of it.

Or—the iceman with his iron tongs gripping a clear cube in summer
 sunlight—maybe he will know.

CARL SANDBURG

Love is possible only if two persons communicate with each other from the center of their existence, hence if each one of them experiences himself from the center of his existence. Only in this "central experience" is human reality, only here is aliveness, only here is the basis for love. Love, experienced thus, is a constant challenge; it is not a resting place, but a moving, growing, working together; even whether there is harmony or conflict, joy or sadness, is secondary to the fundamental fact that two people experience themselves from the essence of their existence, that they are one with each other by being one with themselves, rather than by fleeing from themselves. There is only one proof for the presence of love: the depth of the relationship, and the aliveness and strength in each person concerned; this is the fruit by which love is recognized.

ERICH FROMM

"What is *real*?" asked the Rabbit one day, when they were lying side by side near the nursery fender, before Nana came to tidy the room. "Does it mean having things that buzz inside you and a stick-out handle?"

"Real isn't how you are made," said the Skin Horse. "It's a thing that happens to you. When a child loves you for a long, long time, not just to play with, but Really loves you, then you become Real."

"Does it hurt?" asked the Rabbit.

"Sometimes," said the Skin Horse, for he was always truthful. "When you are Real you don't mind being hurt."

"Does it happen all at once, like being wound up," he asked, "or bit by bit?"

"It doesn't happen all at once," said the Skin Horse. "You become. It takes a long time. That's why it doesn't happen often to people who break easily, or have sharp edges, or who have to be carefully kept. Generally, by the time you are Real, most of your hair has been loved off, and your eyes drop out and you get all loose in the joints and very shabby. But these things don't matter at all, because once you are Real you can't be ugly, except to people who don't understand."

MARGERY WILLIAMS

Our love has been anything but perfect and anything but static. Inevitably there have been times when one of us has outrun the other and has had to wait patiently for the other to catch up. There have been times when we have misunderstood each other, demanded too much of each other, been insensitive to the other's needs. I do not believe there is any marriage where this does not happen. The growth of love is not a straight line, but a series of hills and valleys. I suspect that in every good marriage there are times when love seems to be over. Sometimes these desert lines are simply the only way to the next oasis, which is far more lush and beautiful after the desert crossing than it could possibly have been without it.

MADELEINE L'ENGLE

Mature love, the love that grows in a committed relationship, does not come from romantic dinners and champagne. It is forged in fire, through the trials, the boredom, the shared tears and laughter, the decisions and doubts and debts of life together. It takes work and the willingness to extend yourself beyond your own skin, taking into account that you are not one, no matter how romantic that may sound. You are two, with different thoughts and desires, customs, dislikes, and expectations. And if you can still meet each other with all those differences, you will know true love. If, instead of giving yourself up to the other, you extend yourself to meet the other, you will have a basis for life together.

JACKIE CLEMENT

While we acknowledge our mutual affection by publicly assuming the relationship of husband and wife, yet, in justice to ourselves and a great principle, we deem it a duty to declare that this act on our part implies no sanction of, nor promise of voluntary obedience to, such of the present laws of marriage as refuse to recognize the wife as an independent, rational being, while they confer upon the husband an injurious and unnatural superiority, investing him with legal power which no honorable man would exercise, and which no man should possess. We protest especially against the laws which give to the husband:

1. The custody of the wife's person.
2. The exclusive control and guardianship of their children.

3. The sole ownership of her personal and use of her real estate, unless previously settled upon her, or placed in the hands of trustees, as in the case of minors, lunatics, and idiots.
4. The absolute right to the product of her industry.
5. Also against laws which give to the widower so much larger and more permanent an interest in the property of his deceased wife than they give to the widow in that of the deceased husband.
6. Finally, against the whole system by which "the legal existence of the wife is suspended during marriage," so that, in most States, she neither has a legal part in the choice of her residence, nor can she make a will, nor sue or be sued in her own name, nor inherit property.

We believe that personal independence and equal human rights can never be forfeited, except for crime; that marriage should be an equal and permanent partnership, and so recognized by law; that until it is so recognized, married partners should provide against the radical injustice of present laws, by every means in their power.

We believe that, where domestic difficulties arise, no appeal should be made to legal tribunals under existing laws, but that all difficulties should be submitted to the equitable adjustment of arbitrators mutually chosen.

Thus, reverencing law, we enter our earnest protest against rules and customs which are unworthy of the name, since they violate justice, the essence of all law.

LUCY STONE AND HENRY BLACKWELL

"Still," he said, "there are a few rules I know to be true about love and marriage: If you don't respect the other person, you're gonna have a lot of trouble. If you don't know how to compromise, you're gonna have a lot of trouble. If you can't talk openly about what goes on between you, you're gonna have a lot of trouble. And if you don't have a common set of values in life, you're gonna have a lot of trouble. Your values must be alike.

"And the biggest one of those values, Mitch?"

Yes?

"Your belief in the *importance* of your marriage."

He sniffed, then closed his eyes for a moment.

"Personally," he sighed, his eyes still closed, "I think marriage is a very important thing to do, and you're missing a hell of a lot if you don't try it."

He ended the subject by quoting the poem he believed in like a prayer: "Love each other or perish."

MITCH ALBOM

Why are we offended when we discover the flowers in the restaurant are plastic? Perhaps because they've fooled us, but more than that I think it's because plastic flowers are intended to last forever. We bring cut flowers into our lives to keep us in touch with the "now"; we give them our immediate attention for we know that they will soon fade and be gone. Billie Barbara and I have come to believe that "Till death do us part" does not mean the relationship will last forever. Quite the contrary, it means death is going to part us, either a personal death or the death of the relationship. The bouquet must be enjoyed, in fact can only be enjoyed, today.

RIC MASTEN

And still one thing remains to furnish the house beautiful,—the most important thing of all, without which guests and books and flowers and pictures and harmonies of color only emphasize the fact that the house is not a home. I mean the warm light in the rooms that comes from kind eyes, from quick unconscious smiles, from gentleness in tones, from little unpremeditated caresses of manner, from habits of fore-thoughtfulness for one another,—all that happy illumination which, on the inside of a house, corresponds to morning sunlight outside falling on quiet dewy fields. It is an atmosphere really generated of many self-controls, of much forbearance, of training in self-sacrifice; but by the time it reaches instinctive expression these stern generators of it are hidden in the radiance resulting. It is like a constant love-song without words, whose meaning is, "We are glad that we are alive together." It is a low pervading music, felt, not heard, which begins each day with the good-morning, and only ends in the dream-drowse beyond good-night. It is cheer; it is peace; it is trust, it is delight; it is all these for, and all these in, each other. It knows no moods—this warm love-light,—but is an even cheer, an even trust. The little festivals of love are kept, but, after all, the best days are the every-days, because they are the every-days of love. The variant dispositions in the members of the home, the elements of personality to be "allowed for," add stimulus and exhilaration to this atmosphere. Shared memories make part of it, shared hopes and fears, shared sorrows; shared self-denials make a very dear part of it.

WILLIAM CHANNING GANNETT

Love is a paradox. It is a deep connection with another person that we know will one day come to an end. Love is a risk, and it requires faith as deep and as committed as any order of monks or nuns might ask of us. But if love entails loss as well as joy, then one fact becomes very clear: To love is perhaps the most courageous thing a human being can ever do. To be vulnerable with another person, to be open enough to let someone into the inner sanctum of our hearts, is an incredibly brave act. Knowing that either breaking up, divorce, or the death of the beloved is inevitable, it is remarkable and noble that any of us try love at all.

To love means to trust the world. To have faith in it, and at least on some level, to have faith in the world. To love someone is to proclaim your faith in life. To have children is to proclaim your trust in the future, because while you will be there in the beginning of that child's life, you will probably not be around for all of it. That you must leave for the future. Love for anyone is perhaps the most religious act imaginable.

JOSHUA SNYDER

I will reveal to you a love potion, without medicine, without herbs, without any witch's magic; if you want to be loved, then Love.

HECATON OF RHODES

Our love of love and our high expectations that it will somehow make life complete seem to be an integral part of the experience. Love seems to promise that life's gaping wounds will close up and heal. It makes little difference that in the past love has shown itself to be painful and disturbing. There is something self-renewing in love. Like the goddesses of Greece, it is able to renew its virginity in a bath of forgetfulness.

I suppose we do learn some things about love each time we experience it. In the failure of a relationship we resolve never to make the same mistakes again. We get toughened to some extent and perhaps become a little wiser. But love itself is eternally young and always manifests some of the folly of youth. So, maybe it is better not to become too jaded by love's suffering and dead ends, but rather to appreciate that emptiness is part of love's heritage and therefore its very nature. It isn't necessary to make strong efforts to avoid past mistakes or to learn how to be clever about love. The advance we make after we have been devastated by love may be to be able simply to enter it freely once again, in spite of our suspicions, to draw ever closer to the darkness and hollowness that are mysteriously necessary in love.

THOMAS MOORE

I gave myself to him,
And took himself for pay.
The solemn contract of a life
Was ratified this way.

The wealth might disappoint,
Myself a poorer prove
Than this great purchaser suspect,
The daily own of Love

Depreciate the vision;
But, till the merchant buy,
Still fable, in the isles of spice,
The subtle cargoes lie.

At least, 't is mutual risk,—
Some found it mutual gain;
Sweet debt of Life,—each night to owe,
Insolvent, every noon.

EMILY DICKINSON

Conquered

O pale! O vivid! dear!
　　O disillusioned eyes
Forever near!
　　O Dream, arise!

I will not turn away
　　From the face I loved again;
Your beauty may sway
　　My life with pain.

I will drink the wine you pour,
　　I will seek to put asunder
Our ways no more—
　　O Love! O Wonder!

ZOË AKINS

The essence of a good marriage is respect for each other's personality combined with that deep intimacy, physical, mental, and spiritual, which makes a serious love between man and woman the most fructifying of all human experiences. Such love, like everything that is great and precious, demands its own morality, and frequently entails a sacrifice of the less to the greater; but such sacrifice must be voluntary, for, where it is not, it will destroy the very basis of the love for the sake of which it is made.

BERTRAND RUSSELL

Well, the real word, I think, is "ordeal," in its proper sense. That is the submission of the individual to something superior to itself. The real life of a marriage or of a true love affair is in the relationship, which is where you are, too. . . .

Like the yin/yang symbol, you see. Here I am, and here she is, and here we are. Now when I have to make a sacrifice, I'm not sacrificing to her, I'm sacrificing to the relationship. Resentment against the other one is wrongly placed. Life is in the relationship, that's where your life now is. That's what a marriage is—whereas, in a love affair, you have two lives in a more or less successful relationship to each other for a certain length of time, as long as it seems agreeable.

JOSEPH CAMPBELL

Valentines

I have a piano in my house that I rarely play. When I practice, which is usually twenty minutes a week, I feel a mixture of frustration and enjoyment. Although I tell myself that I'd like to play better, I don't give music an important place in my life. Sometimes I wish I didn't even own a piano. Whenever I have fantasies about living in a rustic cabin in the woods, the piano feels like an anchor and impediment to my freedom. But a piano is a nice piece of furniture. Owning it gives me a sense of settledness and solidity.

Many of us have relationships that are like pianos. They become part of the furniture of our existence. We may have purchased our pianos or begun our relationships with a sense of high ambition and excitement. We dreamed of making beautiful music together. Now we've settled into a routine of plodding mediocrity.

Becoming a better lover is like becoming a better piano player. It's partly in the fingers and partly in the soul, but there is one principle common to both—to give it a place of priority in our lives. Twenty minutes a week is not enough time to become a Horowitz or Scott Joplin, nor is it enough time to build intimacy, trust, and camaraderie with another person. Whether you aim to make it to Carnegie Hall or to have a good relationship, the rule is the same. You need more than passion. The art of loving, like mastering the keyboard, takes practice, practice, practice.

GARY A. KOWALSKI

After a little more than a quarter century of "marital bliss," my tentative conclusion is that two people must want to share basic things out of life, for themselves and for each other, to have a successful marriage.

And it is my opinion that most people enter marriage without giving this matter the consideration it deserves.

Of course, people's minds change or time passes, but this is usually because they weren't on firm footing to begin with.

And, of course, for some, it takes a long time to recognize what they want. But indecision early on is much to be preferred over a false sureness at the start that later ends in confusion.

My only advice here is to be sure what you want because you will probably get it.

DICK ERNST

Love is hard work. There is a myth prevalent in our culture that we should be able to fall in love with someone and then live happily ever after. One of the greatest mistakes that young lovers make—and young lovers can include folks who are past middle age, is believing that a lifelong partnership should be easy, light, and joyful the vast majority of the time.

Real love is more than the magic spell of romantic love that inevitably wears off. Anybody who gets married will in time be confronted by a beloved who is as confused, limited, and full of weakness as each and every one of us. Only then, when you look on another's humanity through the lens of your own, does the opportunity of truly loving reveal itself.

ALAN TAYLOR

That Love May Grow

That I may hear your words,
Listen to mine.
That I may know your heart,
Speak to mine.
That I may follow your dreams,
Share mine.
That I may grow in love,
Grow with mine.
That I may share your life,
Give me time.

MELINDA MORRIS PERRIN

But marriage is marriage, you know. Marriage is not a love affair. A love affair is a totally different thing. A marriage is a commitment to that which you are. That person is literally your other half. And you and the other are one. A love affair isn't that. That is a relationship for pleasure, and when it gets to be unpleasurable, it's off. But a marriage is a life commitment, and a life commitment means the prime concern of your life. If marriage is not the prime concern, you're not married.

JOSEPH CAMPBELL

It's no good trying to fool yourself about love. You can't fall into it like a soft job, without dirtying up your hands. It takes muscle and guts. And if you can't bear the thought of messing up your nice, clean soul, you'd better give up the whole idea of life, and become a saint. Because you'll never make it as a human being. It's either this world or the next.

JOHN OSBORNE

When two people are under the influence of the most violent, most insane, most delusive, and most transient of passions, they are required to swear that they will remain in that excited, abnormal, and exhausting condition until death do them part.

GEORGE BERNARD SHAW

Love is a temporary madness, it erupts like volcanoes and then sub-sides. And when it subsides you have to make a decision. You have to work out whether your roots have so entwined together that it is inconceivable that you should ever part. Because this is what love is. Love is not breathlessness, it is not excitement, it is not the promulga-tion of promises of eternal passion, it is not the desire to mate every second minute of the day, it is not lying awake at night imagining that he is kissing every cranny of your body. No, don't blush, I am telling you some truths. That is just being "in love," which any fool can do. Love itself is what is left over when being in love has burned away, and this is both an art and a fortunate accident. Your mother and I had it, we had roots that grew towards each other underground, and when all the pretty blossoms had fallen from our branches we found that we were one tree and not two.

LOUIS DE BERNIÈRES

Camerado, I give you my hand!
I give you my love, more precious than money,
I give you myself, before preaching or law;
Will you give me yourself? will you come travel with me?
Shall we stick by each other as long as we live?

WALT WHITMAN

Sometimes our life reminds me
of a forest in which there is a graceful clearing
and in that opening a house,
an orchard and garden,
comfortable shades, and flowers
red and yellow in the sun, a pattern
made in the light for the light to return to.
The forest is mostly dark, its ways
to be made anew day after day, the dark
richer than the light and more blessed,
provided we stay brave
enough to keep on going in.

WENDELL BERRY

Come, let us plant our love as farmers plant
A seed, and you shall water it with tears,
And I shall weed it with my hands until
They bleed. Perchance this buried love of ours
Will fall on goodly ground and bear a tree
With fruit and flowers.

COUNTEE CULLEN

Slowly the new home grows holy as the deepening wedding thus goes on; holy, for the making of two souls—two yet one—is going on in it. Each soul is overcoming its own faults for love's sake, and helping by love to overcome the other's faults. Business, sorrows, joys, temptations, failures, victories, ideals, are all shared in it. By and by the awes of motherhood and fatherhood are shared, and the new co-education that children bring their parents is entered on together. The supreme beauty is attained when both realize that the inmost secret of true marriage is—to love the ideals better than each other.

WILLIAM CHANNING GANNETT

I'm asked with increasing frequency, "But why marry?" a question to be taken seriously, especially when it comes from young people who have seen their parents' marriages end in divorce, or in constant bickering and hostility, which is almost worse. The desire to make sure that there is integrity in love, that neither partner wants to use or manipulate the other, is a healthy one. But ultimately there comes a moment when a decision must be made. Ultimately two people who love each other must ask themselves how much they hope for as their love grows and deepens, and how much risk they are willing to take.

MADELEINE L'ENGLE

In any marriage, even a good marriage, there are likely to emerge some amazing diversities and disquieting incompatibilities. Two persons do not come into the marriage relationship like newly hatched chicks. Each partner in the marriage has a history and a family of his own; different habit patterns and social patterns and different family relationship patterns. These patterns must now be brought together, mutually adjusted—in many instances merged—and the merging is not a process that can be completed in a day, or week, or year, or even in a lifetime.

What then? A lingering, haunting maladjustment? Too much concession by one of the partners and too little or none at all by the other? Or a mutual probing of ways and means by which that alienation can be either broken down or bridged over without the sacrifice of dignity or integrity by either? It is easy to just say these words; but to give them meaning and substance is to master the difficult art of living a life that is truly shared. In society at large it is called democracy; in the intimacies of marriage and the home, it is known as love. To some extent each life of the marriage partnership must be identified with that of the other, without possession or ownership—each recognizing the other's strength and weakness, each complementing and supporting the other.

EDWIN T. BUEHRER

The Puritans called marriage "the little church within the Church." In marriage, every day you love, and every day you forgive. It is an ongoing sacrament—love and forgiveness.

BILL MOYERS

The Third Body

A man and a woman sit near each other, and they do not long
At this moment to be older, or younger, or born
In any other nation, or any other time, or any other place.
They are content to be where they are, talking or not talking.
Their breaths together feed someone whom we do not know.
The man sees the way his fingers move;
He sees her hands close around a book she hands to him.
They obey a third body that they share in common.
They have promised to love that body.
Age may come; parting may come; death will come!
A man and a woman sit near each other;
As they breathe they feed someone we do not know,
Someone we know of, whom we have never seen.

ROBERT BLY

The marriage relationship is among the most intense of experiences, but its intensity will burn away rather than multiply the convergent energies of the partners if equality is not its mainspring.

KHOREN ARISIAN

That was enough
for me to forgive you.
To spirit a tiger
from its cell.

Called me *corazón*
in that instant before
I let go the phone
back to its cradle.

Your voice small.
Heat of your eyes,
how I would've placed
my mouth on each.

Said *corazón*
and the word blazed
like a branch of *jacaranda*.

SANDRA CISNEROS

Let It Be a Dance

Let it be a dance we do.
May I have this dance with you?
Through the good times
And the bad times, too,
Let it be a dance.

Let a dancing song be heard.
Play the music say the words,
Fill the sky with sailing birds.
Let it be a dance.
Learn to follow, learn to lead,
Feel the rhythm, fill the need.
To reap the harvest, plant the seed.
And let it be a dance.

Everybody turn and spin,
Let your body learn to bend,
and, like a willow with the wind,
Let it be a dance.

A child is born, the old must die,
A time for joy, a time to cry.
Take it as it passes by.
And let it be a dance.

Morning star comes out at night,
Without the dark there is no light.
If nothing's wrong, then nothing's right.
Let it be a dance.
Let the sun shine, let it rain,
Share the laughter, bare the pain,
And round and round we go again.
Let it be a dance.

RIC MASTEN

Love without marriage can sometimes be very awkward for all concerned; but marriage without love simply removes that institution from the territory of the humanly admissible, to my mind. Love is a state in which one lives who loves, and whoever loves has given himself away; love then, and not marriage, is belonging. Marriage is the public declaration of a man and a woman that they have formed a secret alliance, with the intention to belong to, and share with each other, a mystical estate; mystical exactly in the sense that the real experience cannot be communicated to others, nor explained even to oneself on rational grounds.

KATHERINE ANNE PORTER

One of my favorite kinds of dancing is called contra dancing. Contra refers to the tension in the dance between pulling close to your partner and pushing away from or against him or her. In one of the steps, called the swing, you stand with your partner and while you push against each other with one hand, you pull close the other hand around the other person's waist. Then you start spinning. As you get more comfortable with each other, you lean your bodies further and further away. The dance gets faster and smoother and more exciting the further apart you can get without losing your grip. When two good dancers get together they lean into each other's hands, they throw back their heads, and they whirl like dervishes, their hair flowing behind them, big smiles on their faces, all the while holding tight and pushing away.

And so I leave you with this image of the whirling couple, whose joy and grace is found somewhere in the tension between push and pull, between holding on and letting go. While we're learning the dance, we're likely to step on each other's toes once in a while. We may fall down. But one day, I pray, we will find the balance necessary to let our love whirl on and on and on. May it be so.

Robert Hardies

Love is knotted and gnarled, like an old tree fighting with the wind, like branches too brittle for their own good, like roots that relentlessly inform how deeply we can trust and how freely we can forgive.

JAN CARLSSON-BULL

Beyond the element of giving, the active character of love becomes evident in the fact that it always implies certain basic elements. These are care, responsibility, respect, and knowledge.

ERICH FROMM

When you love you should not say, "God is in my heart," but rather, "I am in the heart of God."

And think not you can direct the course of love, for love, if it finds you worthy, directs your course.

Love has no other desire but to fulfill itself.

But if you love and must needs have desires, let these be your desires:

To melt and be like a running brook that sings its melody to the night.

To know the pain of too much tenderness.

To be wounded by your own understanding of love;

And to bleed willingly and joyfully.

To wake at dawn with a winged heart and give thanks for another day of loving;

To rest at the noon hour and meditate love's ecstasy;

To return home at eventide with gratitude;

And then to sleep with a prayer for the beloved in your heart and a song of praise upon your lips.

Kahlil Gibran

Love not me for comely grace,
For my pleasing eye or face,
Nor for any outward part,
No, nor for a constant heart:
    For these may fail or turn to ill,
      So thou and I shall sever:
Keep, therefore, a true woman's eye,
And love me still but know not why—
    So hast thou the same reason still
      To doat upon me ever!

ANONYMOUS

Love is so strong a thing,
The very gods must yield,
When it is welded fast
With the unflinching truth.

Love is so frail a thing,
A word, a look, will kill.
Oh lovers, have a care
How ye do deal with love.

BLISS CARMAN

If you to me be cold,
　　Or I be false to you,
The world will go on, I think,
　　Just as it used to do;
The clouds will flirt with the moon,
　　The sun will kiss the sea,
The wind to the trees will whisper,
　　And laugh at you and me;
But the sun will not shine so bright,
The clouds will not seem so white,
　　To one, as they will to two;
So I think you had better be kind,
　　And I had best be true,
And let the old love go on,
　　Just as it used to do.

WILL CARLETON

I knew a couple happily married for over fifty years. At their anniversary celebration, they were asked to reflect on their many years of married life. The wife said, "I regret the time we wasted trying to improve each other." The husband said, "The secret of my marital success is I wake up every morning, look in the mirror and say to myself 'You're no prize either.'"

MARY PIPHER

The emotion of love, in spite of the romantics, is not self-sustaining; it endures only when the lovers love many things together, and not merely each other.

WALTER LIPPMANN

This Is Just to Say

I have eaten
the plums
that were in
the icebox

and which
you were probably
saving
for breakfast

Forgive me
they were delicious
so sweet
and so cold

WILLIAM CARLOS WILLIAMS

This May Be All We Need

Here in the space between us and the world
lies human meaning.

Into the vast uncertainty we call.

The echoes make our music,
sharp equations which can hold the stars,
and marvelous mythologies we trust.

This may be all we need
to lift our love against indifference and pain.

Here in the space between us and each other
lies all the future
of the fragment of the universe
which is our own.

RAYMOND JOHN BAUGHAN

What do we live for, if it is not to make life less difficult to each other?

GEORGE ELIOT

Is love, then, so simple my dear?
　　The opening of a door,
And seeing all things clear?
　　I did not know before.

I had thought it unrest and desire
　　Soaring only to fall,
Annihilation and fire:
　　It is not so at all.

I feel no desperate will,
　　But I think I understand
Many things, as I sit quite still,
　　With Eternity in my hand.

IRENE RUTHERFORD MCLEOD

And Ruth said, Intreat me not to leave thee, or to return from following after thee: for whither thou goest, I will go; and where thou lodgest, I will lodge: thy people shall be my people, and thy God my God:

　　Where thou diest, will I die, and there will I be buried: the Lord do so to me, and more also, if ought but death part thee and me.

RUTH 1:16–17

Peace

Peace flows into me
    As the tide to the pool by the shore;
    It is mine forevermore,
It will not ebb like the sea.

I am the pool of blue
    That worships the vivid sky;
    My hopes were heaven-high,
They are all fulfilled in you.

I am the pool of gold
    When sunset burns and dies—
    You are my deepening skies;
Give me your stars to hold.

Sara Teasdale

Oh, the comfort—the inexpressible comfort of feeling *safe* with a person—having neither to weigh thoughts nor measure words, but pouring them all right out, just as they are, chaff and grain together; certain that a faithful hand will take and sift them, keep what is worth keeping, and then with the breath of kindness blow the rest away.

Dinah Craik

He Wishes for the Cloths of Heaven

Had I the heavens' embroidered cloths,
Enwrought with golden and silver light,
The blue and the dim and the dark cloths
Of night and light and the half-light,
I would spread the cloths under your feet:
But I, being poor, have only my dreams;
I have spread my dreams under your feet;
Tread softly because you tread on my dreams.

WILLIAM BUTLER YEATS

"What does that mean— 'tame'?"

"It is an act too often neglected," said the fox. "It means to establish ties."

"'To establish ties'?"

"Just that," said the fox. "To me, you are still nothing more than a little boy who is just like a hundred thousand other little boys. And I have no need of you. And you, on your part, have no need of me. To you, I am nothing more than a fox like a hundred thousand other foxes. But if you tame me, then we shall need each other. To me, you will be unique in all the world. To you, I shall be unique in all the world. . . ."

"I am beginning to understand," said the little prince. "There is a flower . . . I think that she has tamed me. . . ."

". . . But if you tame me, it will be as if the sun came to shine on my life. I shall know the sound of a step that will be different from all the others. Other steps send me hurrying back underneath the ground. Yours will call me, like music, out of my burrow. And then look: you see the grain-fields down yonder? I do not eat bread. Wheat is of no use to me. The wheat fields have nothing to say to me. And that is sad. But you have hair that is the color of gold. Think how wonderful that will be when you have tamed me! The grain, which is also golden, will bring me back the thought of you. And I shall love to listen to the wind in the wheat . . ."

ANTOINE DE ST. EXUPÉRY

Misgivings

"Perhaps you'll tire of me," muses
my love, although she's like a great city
to me, or a park that finds new
ways to wear each flounce of light
and investiture of weather.
Soil doesn't tire of rain, I think,

but I know what she fears: plans warp,
planes explode, topsoil gets peeled away
by floods. And worse than what we can't
control is what we could; those drab,

scuttled marriages we shed so
gratefully may augur we're on our own

for good reasons. "Hi honey," chirps Dread
when I come through the door, "you're home."
Experience is a great teacher
of the value of experience,
its claustrophobic prudence,
its gloomy name-the-disasters-

in-advance charisma. Listen,
my wary one, it's far too late
to unlove each other. Instead let's cook
something elaborate and not
invite anyone to share it but eat it
all up very very slowly.

WILLIAM MATTHEWS

Marriage is about human happiness; the joy of giving and receiving love. It's about standing together, facing whatever life brings, and knowing that despite sorrow and disappointment, your willingness to support and encourage one another will help bring you through hard times.

Marriage is about the work of self-discovery and coming to know your partner's deepest hopes, fears, and pleasures. It is the lifelong process of revealing your own needs and feelings to someone you trust and of living with the changing needs and feelings of your partner.

Marriage is an opportunity to create a space of emotional safety, trust, and connection that nourishes each partner's heart and spirit.

Or as one couple remarked, "Marriage is having a friend who loves you as you are, who trusts you and helps you find the best in yourself through honesty and openness."

CHRISTINE BROWNLIE

What greater thing is there for two human souls, than to feel that they are joined for life—to strengthen each other in all labour, to rest on each other in all sorrow, to minister to each other in all pain, to be one with each other in silent unspeakable memories at the moment of the last parting?

GEORGE ELIOT

Love requires us to approach another person, a person different from ourselves, a person in whom we see amazing possibilities, and to trust that person with our happiness and well-being. With that person, a stranger at first, we both lose ourselves and, if all goes well, find ourselves.

LYNN STRAUSS

Still, the way it happened to me, when I was up against it, you know, hapless, damaged, looking into the void, it was as if Whoever Is in Charge Here said, "This man needs *that* good woman in his life." Not *"a* good woman"—of which there has never been a shortage. But *"that* good woman"—of whom there is this only one.

That's what made it seem, well, personal—a personal save—the one with my name on it since the beginning of time just waiting for me to walk in out of the blue and say I'm ready now.

Mind you, we had both spent many years, all of our lives, really, demonstrating our ability to live without each other. And each of us brought a fair bit of "baggage." And each of us could survive, maybe even thrive, without the other. And no one knows what the future holds.

But when I look into her eyes I see the blindness of love. That's the gift. It is not darkness. It is a vision. She sees me in the way Whoever Is in Charge Here meant me to be seen. She sees me better than I see myself.

THOMAS LYNCH

How Is It That I love You?

I was lost in hopeless loneliness;
I was afraid and bitter and empty.
Every beat of my heart
Fell, shattering, to the ground.

And then you touched me.

I opened like a flower opens
When it feels the sun on its face.
I filled like a dry pool
Filling with cool rain.
You wandered around in my heart,
And I was not alone.

I love you with a love like a river
That flows with water running
Together from two springs.

KEN COLLIER

My true love hath my heart, and I have his,
By just exchange, one for the other given.
I hold his dear, and mine he cannot miss:
There never was a better bargain driven.
His heart in me, keeps me and him in one,
My heart in him, his thoughts and senses guides:
He loves my heart, for once it was his own:
I cherish his, because in me it bides.

Sir Philip Sidney

A Woman's Beloved

To what shall a woman liken her beloved,
And with what shall she compare him to do him honor?
He is like the close-folded new leaves of the woodbine, odorless, but
    sweet,
Flushed with a new and swiftly rising life,
Strong to grow and give glad shade in summer.
Even thus should a woman's beloved shelter her in time of anguish.

And he is like the young robin, eager to try his wings,
For within soft-stirring wings of the spirit has she cherished him,
And with the love of the mother bird shall she embolden him, that
    his flight may avail.
A woman's beloved is to her as the roots of the willow,

Long, strong, white roots, bedded lovingly in the dark.
Into the depths of her have gone the roots of his strength and of his pride,
That she may nourish him well and become his fulfilment.
None may tear him from the broad fields where he is planted!

A woman's beloved is like the sun rising upon the waters, making the
    dark places light,
And like the morning melody of the pine trees.
Truly, she thinks the roses die joyously
If they are crushed beneath his feet.
A woman's beloved is to her a great void that she may illumine,
A great king that she may crown, a great soul that she may redeem.
And he is also the perfecting of life,
Flowers for the altar, bread for the lips, wine for the chalice.

You that have known passion, think not that you have fathomed love.
It may be that you have never seen love's face.
For love thrusts aside storm-clouds of passion to unveil the heavens,
And, in the heart of a woman, only then is love born.

To what shall I liken a woman's beloved,
And with what shall I compare him to do him honor?
He is a flower, a song, a struggle, a wild storm,
And, at the last, he is redemption, power, joy, fulfilment and perfect
    peace.

MARGUERITE WILKINSON

Love (III)

Love bade me welcome, yet my soul drew back,
    Guilty of dust and sin.
But quick-ey'd Love, observing me grow slack
    From my first entrance in,
Drew nearer to me, sweetly questioning
    If I lack'd anything.

"A guest," I answer'd, "worthy to be here";
    Love said, "You shall be he."
"I, the unkind, the ungrateful? ah my dear,
    I cannot look on thee."
Love took my hand and smiling did reply,
    "Who made the eyes but I?"

"Truth, Lord, but I have marr'd them; let my shame
    Go where it doth deserve."
"And know you not," says Love, "who bore the blame?"
    "My dear, then I will serve."
"You must sit down," says Love, "and taste my meat."
    So I did sit and eat.

GEORGE HERBERT

Cornucopia

Always before
there was the holding back:

don't show your love too much
or he will run away.

Give the words like little gifts
& never say:

I love you
too soon, too soon.

Anytime was always
much too soon.

But I heaped you with love
& you kept on coming back.

And I talked and talked and talked
& you kept on talking back.

And I heaped my love on you
& you kept on heaping yours.

What did you think we were *holding*
by holding back?

Why did we think it *safe*
to hoard our love?

The cornucopia returns
upon itself.

The fruits fall out.
We eat them & they grow.

ERICA JONG

Variation on the Word Sleep

I would like to watch you sleeping,
which may not happen.
I would like to watch you,
sleeping. I would like to sleep
with you, to enter
your sleep as its smooth dark wave
slides over my head

and walk with you through that lucent
wavering forest of bluegreen leaves
with its watery sun & three moons
towards the cave where you must descend,
towards your worst fear

I would like to give you the silver
branch, the small white flower, the one
word that will protect you
from the grief at the center
of your dream, from the grief
at the center. I would like to follow
you up the long stairway
again & become
the boat that would row you back
carefully, a flame
in two cupped hands
to where your body lies
beside me, and you enter
it as easily as breathing in

I would like to be the air
that inhabits you for a moment
only. I would like to be that unnoticed
& that necessary.

Margaret Atwood

When two individuals meet, so do two private worlds. None of our private worlds is big enough for us to live a wholesome life in. We need the wider world of joy and wonder, of purpose and venture, of toil and tears. What are we, any of us, but strangers and sojourners forlornly wandering through the nighttime until we draw together and find the meaning of our lives in one another, dissolving our fears in each other's courage, making music together and lighting torches to guide us through the dark? We belong together. Love is what we need. To love and to be loved. Let our hearts be open; and what we would receive from others, let us give. For what is given still remains to bless the giver—when the gift is love.

A. POWELL DAVIES

Honesty, forgiveness and devotion—my holy trinity of marital virtues. It has to be more than "he makes me feel good about myself," because that will pass. It has to be about some commitment to each other's personal and spiritual well-being, a covenant to bring the other fully into the world. And in so doing, all loving relationships become the vehicle for what is quite extraordinary and simply divine.

VANESSA SOUTHERN

As long as human beings people the earth,
We can be assured
That in our loneliness
There is also love—
Deep, infinite love,
Waiting to be tapped,
To water the barren brown lawn of our loneliness—
Love which shrivels if kept to the self,
Which flourishes only if it is given away.

I need you.
You need me.
I know it.
You know it.
What are we waiting for?

RICHARD S. GILBERT

An honorable human relationship—that is, one in which two people have the right to use the word "love"—is a process, delicate, violent, often terrifying to both persons involved, a process of refining the truths they can tell each other.

It is important to do this because it breaks down human self-delusion and isolation.

It is important to do this because in so doing we do justice to our own complexity.

It is important to do this because we can count on so few people to go that hard way with us.

ADRIENNE RICH

After Parting

Oh, I have sown my love so wide
    That he will find it everywhere;
It will awake him in the night,
    It will enfold him in the air.

I set my shadow in his sight
    And I have winged it with desire,
That it may be a cloud by day,
    And in the night a shaft of fire.

SARA TEASDALE

Let me not to the marriage of true minds
Admit impediments. Love is not love
Which alters when it alteration finds,
Or bends with the remover to remove:
O, no! it is an ever-fixèd mark
That looks on tempests and is never shaken;
It is the star to every wandering bark,
Whose worth's unknown, although his height be taken.
Love's not Time's fool, though rosy lips and cheeks
Within his bending sickle's compass come;
Love alters not with his brief hours and weeks,
But bears it out even to the edge of doom.
If this be error, and upon me prov'd,
I never writ, nor no man ever lov'd.

WILLIAM SHAKESPEARE

Two persons love in one another the future good which they aid one
another to unfold.

MARGARET FULLER

Touch Me

Touch is an art
That gets better with practice
Isolation leads to alienation
And you lose your touch

Life without touch
Has no art
Life without art
Has no meaning

Touch me
So I can breathe
Touch me
So I can feel
Touch me
So I can cry
Touch me
So I can live again
Touch me.

MELINDA MORRIS PERRIN

You know what getting married is? It's agreeing to take this person who is right now at the top of his form, full of hopes and ideas, feeling good, looking good, wildly interested in you because you're the same way, and sticking by him while he slowly disintegrates. And he does the same for you. You're his responsibility now, and he's yours. If no one else will take care of him, you will. If everyone else rejects you, he won't. What do you think love is? Going to bed all the time? Poo! Don't be weak. Have some spine! He's yours and you're his, he doesn't beat you or abuse you, and you've each made about the same bargain. Now that you know what it's like to be married, now that all the gold leaf has sort of worn off, you can make something of it, you can really learn to love each other.

JANE SMILEY

Eros, at its best, is deeply entwined with the sacred. Just look at the best of sacred art.

But love is something more than eros, more than pleasure and romance. There is also a deep affection of love; we call that friendship, or philos. Friendship draws us into relationship and companionship. Friendship provides each party with a sense of satisfaction and a reassuring sense of togetherness. Friendship keeps us from feeling alone and lonely. It gives us someone we can trust, someone we can contact when we need to, someone who stands ready to help, someone who understands us, someone who gives us the benefit of the doubt. Friendship is tender and caring and mutually enriching. Philos complements eros. It is more mutual than eros, and sometimes more loyal. Eros is anything but steady and calm. Friendship is steadfast and dependable.

And then there is that devotion that is beyond both pleasure and attraction, beyond eros and philos. It is a devotion rooted in pure commitment. It holds on when pleasure and desire fade, when friendship is strained. It hangs on when times are hard. Dr. King called such love *agape*, the Greek word for truly unselfish love.

All three of these qualities of love are positive and wholesome, and true love is not complete without elements of each; but when the chips are down and the needs are great, it is agape that does the heavy pulling. It is agape that requires strength. It is agape that tests our character to its limits. It is agape that holds on. It is agape that can and will endure pain for the other. It is agape that transcends self-interest. It is agape that knows about reconciliation. It is agape that is large-hearted enough to forgive. It is agape that builds community.

THOMAS MIKELSON

Love is the only way to grasp another human being in the innermost core of his personality. No one can become fully aware of the very essence of another human being unless he loves him. By the spiritual act of love he is enabled to see the essential traits and features in the beloved person; and even more, he sees that which is potential in him, that which is not yet actualized but yet ought to be actualized. Furthermore, by his love, the loving person enables the beloved person to actualize these potentialities. By making him aware of what he can be and of what he should become, he makes these potentialities come true.

VIKTOR FRANKL

Two are better than one, because they have a good reward for their toil. For if they fall, one will lift up his fellow; but woe to him who is alone when he falls and has not another to lift him up. Again, if two lie together, they are warm; but how can one be warm alone?

ECCLESIASTES 4:10–12

The Silver Road

To F. W.

You are my companion
Down the silver road,
Still and many-changing,
Infinitely changing.
You are my companion.
Something sings in lives—
Days of walking on and on,
Deep beyond all singing,
Wonderful past singing.

Wonderful our road,
Long and many-changing,
Infinitely changing.
This, more wonderful—
We are here together,
You and I together,
I am your companion;
You are my companion,
My own, true companion.

Let the road-side fade:
Morning on the mountain-top,
Hours along the valley,
Days of walking on and on,
Pulse away in silence,

In eternal silence.
Let the world all fade,
Break and pass away.
Yet will this remain,
Deep beyond all singing,
My own true companion,
Beautiful past singing:
We were here together—
On this earth together;
I was your companion,
You were my companion,
My own true companion.

EDITH WYATT

The Bean Eaters

They eat beans mostly, this old yellow pair.
Dinner is a casual affair.
Plain chipware on a plain and creaking wood,
Tin flatware.

Two who are Mostly Good.
Two who have lived their day,
But keep on putting on their clothes
And putting things away.

And remembering . . .
Remembering, with twinklings and twinges,
As they lean over the beans in their rented back room that
    is full of
beads and receipts and dolls and cloths, tobacco crumbs,
vases and fringes.

Gwendolyn Brooks

Friendship After Love

After the fierce midsummer all ablaze
    Has burned itself to ashes, and expires
    In the intensity of its own fires,
There come the mellow, mild, St. Martin days
Crowned with the calm of peace, but sad with haze.
    So after Love has led us, till he tires
    Of his own throes, and torments, and desires,
Comes large-eyed friendship: with a restful gaze,
He beckons us to follow, and across
    Cool verdant vales we wander free from care.
    Is it a touch of frost lies in the air?
Why are we haunted with a sense of loss?
We do not wish the pain back, or the heat;
And yet, and yet, these days are incomplete.

Ella Wheeler Wilcox

Words By Heart

We've given my father a microphone
at his 75th birthday party
because singing is the only thing
he still does fluently.

Sing "Where or When," Sandy. I love that.
My mother has had two vodka martinis.

Where or when? he asks.

Yes—the song. Come on, sing it.

Sanford holds onto the mike stand,
listing just a little to the left.
Everyone's quiet, trying not to expect much.
He clears his throat, cranes his neck:

It seems we stood and talked like this before
his blind sister Ruth—with the voice of a stage star—
sits near him, mouthing the words like a nervous parent
we looked at each other in the same way then,
though I can't remember where or when
my mother and my sister Diane are on the couch,
riveted, grave, both of them in green
and *the clothes you're wearing are the clothes*

you wore, the smile you are smiling you were smiling
then there's my brother-in-law and my young niece,
who lean against each other, eyes closed
though I can't remember where or when it's all happening,
silver pooling at its edges as *some things that happen*
for the first time seem to be happening again
my cousin Andrea watches her husband
switch the video camera on, her four-year-old
shifting onto her lap *and so it seems*
that we have met before and laughed before
Uncle Cy and Aunt Bea look up from their hands
as I look down at mine, thinking
this man once wrote songs and speeches and eulogies
and loved before, which everyone here remembers—
even as he sings mechanically, frowning:
even as the lyrics stray from him into the microphone
like exhaust, like a last breath,
but who knows where or when.

JODY BOLZ

the quiet thoughts
of two people a long time in love
touch lightly
like birds nesting in each others warmth
you will know them by their laughter
but to each other
they speak mostly through their silence
if they find themselves apart
they may dream of sitting undisturbed
in each other's presence
of wrapping themselves warmly in each
    other's ease

HUGH PRATHER

A Marriage Ring

The ring, so worn as you behold,
So thin, so pale, is yet of gold:
The passion such it was to prove—
Worn with life's care, love yet was love.

GEORGE CRABBE

We Have Lived and Loved Together

We have lived and loved together
    Through many changing years;
We have shared each other's gladness
    And wept each other's tears;
I have known ne'er a sorrow
    That was long unsoothed by thee;
For thy smiles can make a summer
    Where darkness else would be.

Like the leaves that fall around us
    In autumn's fading hours,
Are the traitor's smiles, that darken
    When the cloud of sorrow lowers;
And though many such we've known, love,
    Too prone, alas, to range,
We both can speak of one love
    Which time can never change.

We have lived and loved together
    Through many changing years,
We have shared each other's gladness
    And wept each other's tears.
And let us hope the future,
    As the past has been will be,

I will share with thee my sorrows,
And thou thy joys with me.

CHARLES JEFFERYS

Love at the closing of our days
is apprehensive and very tender.

FYODOR TYUTCHEV

Often he thought: My life did not begin until I knew her.

She would like to hear this, he was sure, but he did not know how to tell her. In the extremity of passion he cried out in a frantic voice: "I love you!" yet even these words were unsatisfactory. He wished for something else to say. He needed to let her know how deeply he felt her presence while they were lying together during the night, as well as each morning when they awoke and in the evening when he came home. However, he could think of nothing appropriate.

So the years passed, they had three children and accustomed themselves to a life together, and eventually Mr. Bridge decided that his wife should expect nothing more of him. After all, he was an attorney rather than a poet; he could never pretend to be what he was not.

EVAN S. CONNELL

My parents, who were married for forty-five years, had two little inside jokes, which, I now realize, weren't jokes at all but gems of connubial wisdom. Every wedding anniversary, they'd refer to "picking up each other's option" for another year. "Well, I'm going to pick up your father's option," my mother would say. Sometimes she would add, "Next year's bound to be better" or "It was a pretty good year."

And Dad had his January/July code. "Look, kid," he'd say to my mother, "if we can make it to January, we can make it to July."

SARA BAN BREATHNACH

Marriage is the clue to human life, but there is no marriage apart from the wheeling sun and the nodding earth, from the straying of the planets and the magnificence of the fixed stars. Is not a man different, utterly different at dawn, from what he is at sunset? and a woman too? And does not the changing harmony and discord of their variation make the secret music of life?

And is it not so throughout life? A man is different at thirty, at forty, at fifty, at sixty, at seventy: and the woman at his side is different. But is there not some strange conjunction in their differences? Is there not some peculiar harmony, through youth, the period of childbirth, the period of florescence and young children, the period of the woman's change of life, painful yet also a renewal, the period of waning passion but mellowing delight of affection, the dim unequal period of the approach of death, when the man and woman look at one another with the dim apprehension of separation that is not really a separation: is there not, throughout it all, some unseen, unknown interplay of balance, harmony, completion, like some soundless symphony which moves with a rhythm from phase to phase, so different, so very different in the various movements, and yet one symphony, made out of the soundless singing of two strange and incompatible lives, a man's and a woman's?

D. H. LAWRENCE

Love's Apotheosis

Love me. I care not what the circling years
    To me may do.
If, but in spite of time and tears,
    You prove but true.

Love me—albeit grief shall dim mine eyes,
    And tears bedew,
I shall not e'en complain, for then my skies
    Shall still be blue.

Love me, and though the winter snow shall pile,
    And leave me chill,
Thy passion's warmth shall make for me, meanwhile,
    A sun-kissed hill.

And when the days have lengthened into years,
    And I grow old,
Oh, spite of pains and griefs and cares and fears,
    Grow thou not cold.

Then hand and hand we shall pass up the hill,
    I say not down;
That twain go up, of love, who've loved their fill,—
    To gain love's crown.

Love me, and let my life take up thine own,
    As sun the dew.
Come, sit, my queen, for in my heart a throne
    Awaits for you!

PAUL LAURENCE DUNBAR

As the traditional marriage ceremony insists, not everything that we stay to find out will make us happy. The faith, rather, is that by staying, and only by staying, we will learn something of the truth, that the truth is good to know, and that it is always both different and larger than we thought.

WENDELL BERRY

The River-Merchant's Wife: A Letter

While my hair was still cut straight across my forehead
I played about the front gate, pulling flowers.
You came by on bamboo stilts, playing horse;
You walked about my seat, playing with blue plums.
And we went on living in the village of Chokan:
Two small people, without dislike or suspicion.

At fourteen I married My Lord you.
I never laughed, being bashful.
Lowering my head, I looked at the wall.
Called to, a thousand times, I never looked back.

At fifteen I stopped scowling,
I desired my dust to be mingled with yours
Forever and forever, and forever.
Why should I climb the look-out?

At sixteen you departed,
You went into far Ku-to-Yen, by the river of swirling eddies,
And you have been gone five months.
The monkeys make sorrowful noise overhead.
You dragged your feet when you went out.
By the gate now, the moss is grown, the different mosses,
Too deep to clear them away!
The leaves fall early this autumn, in wind.

The paired butterflies are already yellow with August
Over the grass in the west garden—
They hurt me.
I grow older.

If you are coming down through the narrows of the river,
Please let me know beforehand,
    And I will come out to meet you, As far as Cho-fu-Sa.

EZRA POUND

A Decade

When you came, you were like red wine and honey,
And the taste of you burnt my mouth with its sweetness.
Now you are like morning bread,
Smooth and pleasant.
I hardly taste you at all, for I know your savor;
But I am completely nourished.

AMY LOWELL

I suppose one night hundreds of thousands of years ago in a cave by a night fire when one of those shaggy men wakened to gaze over the banked coals at his woman, his children, and thought of their being cold, dead, gone forever. Then he must have wept. And he put out his hand in the night to the woman who must die some day and to the children who must follow her. And for a little bit next morning, he treated them somewhat better, for he saw that they, like himself, had the seed of night in them.

RAY BRADBURY

It is not true that people in long marriages dissolve into each other, becoming one being. I touch Tom's elbow, the sleeve of his tan jacket; he places his long arms around me and his hands cup my breasts in the friendliest possible way. We are two people in a snapshot, but with a little cropping we could each exist on our own. But that's not what we want. Hold the frame still, contain us, the two of us together, that's what we ask for. This is all it takes to keep the world from exploding.

CAROL SHIELDS

When marrying, ask yourself this question: Do you believe that you will be able to converse well with this person into your old age? Everything else in marriage is transitory.

FRIEDRICH NIETZSCHE

It takes years to marry completely two hearts, even of the most loving and well-assorted. A happy wedlock is a long falling in love. Young persons think love belongs only to the brown-haired and crimson-cheeked. So it does for its beginning. But the golden marriage is a part of love which the Bridal day knows nothing of.

A perfect and complete marriage, where wedlock is everything you could ask and the ideal of marriage becomes actual, is not common, perhaps as rare as perfect personal beauty. Men and women are married fractionally, now a small fraction, then a large fraction. Very few are married totally, and they only after some forty or fifty years of gradual approach and experiment.

THEODORE PARKER

Love takes time. What are called "love affairs" may afford a wide, and in retrospect, illuminating variety of emotions; not only fierce satisfactions and swooning delights, but the horrors of jealousy and the desperation of parting attend them; the hangover from one of these emotional riots may be long and dreadful.

But rarely have the pleasures of love an opportunity to manifest themselves in such riots of passion. Love affairs are for emotional sprinters; the pleasures of love are for the emotional marathoners.

ROBERTSON DAVIES

Grow old along with me!
The best is yet to be,
The last of life, for which the first was made:
Our times are in his hand
Who saith, "A whole I planned,
Youth shows but half; trust God: see all, nor be afraid!"

ROBERT BROWNING

The Wedded Lover

I read in our old journals of the days
When our first love was April-sweet and new,
How fair it blossomed and deep-rooted grew
Despite the adverse time; and our amaze
At moon and stars and beauty beyond praise
That burgeoned all about us: gold and blue
The heaven arched us in, and all we knew
Was gentleness. We walked on happy ways.
They said by now the path would be more steep,
the sunsets paler and less mild the air;
Rightly we heeded not; it was not true.
We will not tell the secret—let it keep.
I know not how I thought those days so fair
These being so much fairer, spent with you.

CHRISTOPHER MORLEY

When you are old and gray and full of sleep,
And nodding by the fire, take down this book,
And slowly read, and dream of the soft look
Your eyes had once, and of their shadows deep;

How many loved your moments of glad grace,
And loved your beauty with love false or true;
But one man loved the pilgrim soul in you,
And loved the sorrows of your changing face.

WILLIAM BUTLER YEATS

She is a woman: one in whom
The spring-time of her childish years
Hath never lost its fresh perfume,
Though knowing well that life hath room
For many blights and many tears.

I love her with a love as still
As a broad river's peaceful might,
Which, by high tower and lowly mill,
Seems following its own wayward will,
And yet doth ever flow aright.

JAMES RUSSELL LOWELL

Love changes, and in change is true.

WENDELL BERRY

Love Autumnal

My love will come in autumn-time
When leaves go spinning to the ground
And wistful stars in heaven chime
With the leaves' sound.

Then, we shall walk through dusty lanes
And pause beneath low-hanging boughs,
And there, while soft-hued beauty reigns
We'll make our vows.

Let others seek in spring for sighs
When love flames forth from every seed;
But love that blooms when nature dies
Is love indeed!

OLIVER JENKINS

We have circled and circled till we have arrived home again, we two,
We have voided all but freedom and all but our own joy.

WALT WHITMAN

One word more.
    You see me young: they call me fair:
I think I have a pleasant face,
      And pretty hair.

But by and by my face will fade,
    It must with time, it may with care:
What say you to a wrinkled wife,
      With thin, gray hair?

You care not, you: in youth, or age,
    Your heart is mine, while life endures.
Is it so? Then, Arthur, here's my hand,
      My heart is yours.

RICHARD HENRY STODDARD

Marriage makes us aware of the changes wrought by time, but the new relationship will continue to draw much of its beauty and meaning from the intimate associations of the past.

WILLIAM R. FORTNER

Believe me, if all those endearing young charms,
    Which I gaze on so fondly to-day,
Were to change by to-morrow, and fleet in my arms,
    Like fairy-gifts fading away,
Thou wouldst still be adored, as this moment thou art,
    Let thy loveliness fade as it will,
And around the dear ruin each wish of my heart
    Would entwine itself verdantly still.

It is not while beauty and youth are thine own,
    And thy cheeks unprofaned by a tear,
That the fervor and faith of a soul can be known,
    To which time will but make thee more dear;
No, the heart that has truly loved never forgets,
    But as truly loves on to the close,
As the sunflower turns on her god, when he sets,
    The same look which she turned when he rose.

THOMAS MOORE

My dear wife! remember thou wast the love of my youth, and much the joy of my life; the most beloved, as well as the most worthy of all my earthly comforts: and the reason of that love was more thy inward than thy outward excellencies, which yet were many. God knows, and thou knowest it, I can say it was a match of Providence's making; and God's image in us both was the first thing, and the most amiable and engaging ornament in our eyes.

WILLIAM PENN

Friendship

Two sturdy oaks I mean, which side by side
    Withstand the winter's storm
    And spite of wind and tide,
    Grow up the meadow's pride
    For both are strong

Above they barely touch, but undermined
    Down to their deepest source,
    Admiring you shall find
    Their roots are intertwined
Insep'rably.

HENRY DAVID THOREAU

Sudden Light

I have been here before,
    But when or how I cannot tell:
I know the grass beyond the door,
    The sweet keen smell,
The sighing sound, the lights around the shore.

You have been mine before,—
    How long ago I may not know:
But just when at that swallow's soar
    Your neck turn'd so,
Some veil did fall,—I knew it all of yore.

Has this been thus before?
    And shall not thus time's eddying flight
Still with our lives our love restore
    In death's despite,
And day and night yield one delight once more?

DANTE GABRIEL ROSSETTI

"Would you hold me when my time is come? I am at peace. Do not grieve."

"If I grieve," I said, "it is not for you, but for myself, beloved, for how shall I endure to live without you, who are my love and my life?"

"You are not alone," he said. "I live in my children. "

KAMALA MARKANDAYA

If I am destined to be happy with you here—how short is the longest Life—I wish to believe in immortality—I wish to live with you for ever.

JOHN KEATS

Prayer for a Marriage

When we are old one night and the moon
arcs over the house like an antique
China saucer and the teacup sun

follows somewhere far behind
I hope the stars deepen to a shine
so bright you could read by it

if you liked and the sadnesses
we will have known go away
for awhile—in this hour or two

before sleep—and that we kiss
standing in the kitchen not fighting
gravity so much as embodying

its sweet force, and I hope we kiss
like we do today knowing so much
good is said in this primitive tongue

from the first wild surprising ones
to the lower dizzy ten thousand
infinitely slower ones—and I hope
while we stand there in the kitchen
making tea and kissing, the whistle
of the teapot wakes the neighbors.

STEVE SCAFIDI

Imagine a dim room
down the long hallway of the future
(It helps to have candles here, too).
The shades are drawn. You are in the bed
and around the foot stand
several solemn young people looking
vaguely like the face you shave each day.
She prays in a chair beside you,
her fingers touching your forearm.
They are gnarled and pale as roots—
a hag's fingers.
What hair she has is white and brittle.
Her eyes have all but disappeared
into the flesh of her face.
Her voice grates on your ears
like a child's violin.
Now, if you find her
absolutely essential to the scene,
if the thought of her not being there
feels empty in your stomach
and full in your throat,
then, perhaps, she is the one.

JOSEPH MEREDITH

Habitation

Marriage is not
a house or even a tent

it is before that, and colder:

the edge of the forest, the edge
of the desert
the unpainted stairs
at the back where we squat
outside, eating popcorn

the edge of the receding glacier

where painfully and with wonder
at having survived even
this far

we are learning to make fire

MARGARET ATWOOD

Index of First Lines

Credits

Selections appear on page numbers in bold.

ACKERMAN   *A Natural History of Love* (**25**) by Diane Ackerman, 1994.

ACTON   "I Love Thee" (**79**), in *Poems* by Eliza Acton, 1826.

AKINS   "Conquered" (**99**) by Zoë Akins, in *Poetry 5*, January 1915.

ALBOM   *Tuesdays with Morrie: An Old Man, A Young Man, and Life's Greatest Lesson* (**94**) by Mitch Albom, 1997.

ANDERSON   *Winesburg, Ohio* (**66**) by Sherwood Anderson, 1919.

ANGELOU   "Where We Belong, A Duet" (**60**), in *And Still I Rise* by Maya Angelou. Copyright © 1978 Maya Angelou. Reprinted with the permission of Random House, Inc., and Virago Press, Ltd.

ANONYMOUS   *Great Occasions: Readings for the Celebration of Birth, Coming-of-Age, Marriage, and Death* (**29**), edited by Carl Seaburg, 1998. *The Oxford Book of English Verse: 1250-1900* (**116**), edited by Arthur Quiller-Couch, 1919.

APACHE SONG   Apache song (**42**), translator unknown, in *Weddings from the Heart: Contemporary and Traditional Ceremonies for an Unforgettable Wedding*, edited by Daphne Rose Kingma, 1991.

ARISIAN   *The New Wedding: Creating Your Own Marriage Ceremony* (**110**) by Khoren Arisian, 1974.

ARNOLD "Somewhere" (**12**) by Edwin Arnold, in *The Random House Treasury of Favorite Love Poems*, 1999.

ATWOOD "Variation on the Word Sleep" (**134**), in *Selected Poems II: Poems Selected and New, 1976-1986* by Margaret Atwood, copyright © 1987 by Margaret Atwood, reprinted with the permission of Houghton Mifflin Company and Oxford University Press, all rights reserved. "Habitation" (**172**), in *Selected Poems 1965-1975* by Margaret Atwood, copyright © 1976 by Margaret Atwood, with the permission of Houghton Mifflin Company, Oxford University Press Canada, and Virago Press, Ltd., all rights reserved.

AZTEC POEM Aztec poem (**65**), in *The Book of Love*, edited by Andrew M. Greeley and Mary G. Durkin, 2002.

BARKER Selection (**16**) by Elsa Barker, in *The Oxford Book of English Mystical Verse*, edited by D. H. S. Nicholson and A. H. E. Lee, 1917.

BAUGHAN *The Sound of Silence* (**121**) by Raymond John Baughan, 1965. Used with permission of William Fisher Baughan.

BERNHARDT Selection (**61**) by Sarah Bernhardt, in *Wedding Toasts and Speeches: Finding the Perfect Words*, edited by Jo Packham, 1993.

BERRY "The Country of Marriage" (**106**), in *The Selected Poems of Wendell Berry*, copyright © 1998 by Wendell Berry, reprinted with the permission of Counterpoint Press, a division of Perseus Books, L. L. C. "Poetry and Marriage" (**157**), in *Standing By Words: Essays* by Wendell Berry, 2005. "The Dance" (**164**), in *The Wheel* by Wendell Berry, 1983.

BLY "The Third Body" (**109**), in *Loving a Woman in Two Worlds* by Robert Bly. Copyright © 1985 by Robert Bly. Used with permission of Doubleday, a division of Random House, Inc.

Bodenheim "Poet to His Love" (**51**), in *Minna and Myself* by Maxwell Bodenheim, 1918.

Bolz "The Words We Say" (**81**) by Jody Bolz, in *The G. W. Forum*, Winter 1992. "Words by Heart" (**150**) by Jody Bolz, in *Poet Lore*, Winter 1997. Used with permission of author.

Botley "A Wedding Meditation" (**40**), adapted from Robert Botley, in *Great Occasions: Readings for the Celebration of Birth, Coming-of-Age, Marriage, and Death*, edited by Carl Seaburg, 1998.

Bradbury *Something Wicked This Way Comes* (**160**) by Ray Bradbury, 1962.

Bradstreet "To My Dear and Loving Husband" (**57**), in *Several Poems* by Anne Bradstreet, 1678.

Brainard "Epithalamium" (**30**) by John Gardiner Calkins Brainard, in *An American Anthology, 1787-1900*, edited by Edmund Clarence Stedman, 1900.

Breathnach *Something More: Excavating Your Authentic Self* (**155**) by Sara Ban Breathnach, 1998.

Bridges "My Delight and Thy Delight" (**75**) by Robert Bridges, in *The Oxford Book of English Verse: 1250-1900*, edited by Arthur Quiller-Couch, 1919.

Brontë *Wuthering Heights* (**57**) by Emily Brontë, 1847.

Brooke "The Great Lover" (**13**) by Rupert Brooke, in *Modern British Poetry*, edited by Louis Untermeyer, 1920.

BROOKS   "The Bean Eaters" (**148**), in *Blacks* by Gwendolyn Brooks. Copyright © 1987 by Gwendolyn Brooks. Reprinted by consent of Brooks Permissions.

BROWNING   "Sonnet 43" (**47**), in *Sonnets from the Portuguese* by Elizabeth Barrett Browning, 1850.

BROWNING   "Rabbi Ben Ezra" (**162**) by Robert Browning, in *The Oxford Book of English Mystical Verse*, edited by D. H. S. Nicholson and A. H. E. Lee, 1917.

BROWNLIE   "What Is Marriage For?" (**126**). Used with permission of Christine Brownlie.

BUCK   *To My Daughters, With Love* (**24**) by Pearl S. Buck, 1967.

BUEHRER   "The Institution of Marriage" (**108**), in *The Art of Being* by Edwin T. Buehrer, 1971. Used with permission of Third Unitarian Church of Chicago.

BURNS   "A Red, Red Rose" (**63**) by Robert Burns, in *The Oxford Book of English Verse: 1250-1900*, edited by Arthur Quiller-Couch, 1919.

BYRON   "She Walks in Beauty" (**72**) by George Gordon Lord Byron, in *The Oxford Book of English Verse: 1250-1900*, edited by Arthur Quiller-Couch, 1919.

CAMPBELL   *The Power of Myth* (**100**, **104**) by Joseph Campbell and Bill Moyers, 1988.

CARLETON   "One and Two" (**117**), in *Farm Ballads* by Will Carleton, 1873.

CARLSSON-BULL   "Love and Loving" (**114**). Used with permission of Jan Carlsson-Bull.

CARMAN *Sappho: One Hundred Lyrics* (**14**, **116**) by Bliss Carman, 1907.

CHAUCER "Rondel of Merciless Beauty" (**74**) by Geoffrey Chaucer, in *A Book of Love Poetry*, edited by Jon Stallworthy, 1973.

CHINESE OATH Chinese oath (**52**), in *A Grateful Heart: Daily Blessings for the Evening Meal from Buddha to the Beatles*, edited by M. J. Ryan, 1994.

CHIPPEWA SONG Chippewa song (**67**), in *Wedding Readings: Centuries of Writing and Rituals on Love and Marriage*, edited by Eleanor Munro, 1989.

CISNEROS "You Called Me Corazón" (**110**), in *Loose Woman* by Sandra Cisneros. Copyright © Sandra Cisneros. Published by Vintage Books, a division of Random House, Inc., and originally in hardcover by Alfred A. Knopf, Inc. Used with permission of Susan Bergholz Literary Services, New York. All rights reserved.

CLEMENT "Paper Valentines" (**92**). Used with permission of Jackie Clement.

CLIFTON "blessing the boats (at st. mary's)" (**43**), in *Blessing the Boats: New and Selected Poems, 1988-2000* by Lucille Clifton. Copyright © 1991, 2000 by Lucille Clifton. Reprinted with the permission of BOA Editions, Ltd.

COLERIDGE "Love" (**18**) by Samuel Taylor Coleridge, in *The Oxford Book of English Verse: 1250-1900*, edited by Arthur Quiller-Couch, 1919.

COLLIER "How Is It That I Love You?" (**129**). Used with permission of Ken Collier.

CONNELL *Mr. Bridge* (**154**) by Evan S. Connell, 1969.

CORINTHIANS 1 Corinthians 13 (**26**), New Revised Standard Version.

CRABBE   "A Marriage Ring" (**152**) by George Crabbe, in *The Oxford Book of English Verse: 1250-1900*, edited by Arthur Quiller-Couch, 1919.

CRAIK   *A Life for a Life* (**123**) by Dinah Craik, 1859.

CULLEN   "Words to My Love" (**106**), in *Copper Sun* by Countee Cullen (New York: Harper & Brothers, 1927). Copyrights held by Amistad Research Center. Administered by Thompson and Thompson, New York, NY.

CUMMINGS   "love is more thicker than forget" (**19**). Copyright 1939, © 1967, 1991 by the Trustees for the E. E. Cummings Trust, from *Complete Poems: 1904-1962* by E. E. Cummings, edited by George J. Firmage. Used by permission of Liveright Publishing Corporation.

DAVIES   "When Two Individuals Come Together" (**136**) by A. Powell Davies, in *Great Occasions: Readings for the Celebration of Birth, Coming-of-Age, Marriage, and Death*, edited by Carl Seaburg, 1998. Used with permission of Muriel A. Davies.

DAVIES   "The Pleasures of Love" (**161**), in *The Enthusiasms of Robertson Davies* by Robertson Davies, edited by Judith Skelton Grant, 1979.

DE BEAUVOIR   *The Second Sex* (**13**) by Simone de Beauvoir, 1952.

DE BERNIÈRES   *Captain Corelli's Mandolin* (**105**) by Louis de Bernières, 1995.

DE BORNEILH   Selection (**21**) by Guiraut de Borneilh, in *The Power of Myth* by Joseph Campbell and Bill Moyers, 1988.

DE CHARDIN   *Hymn of the Universe* (**7**) by Pierre Teilhard de Chardin, 1961.

DE SAINT-EXUPÉRY   *The Little Prince* (**15**, **124**) by Antoine de Saint-Exupéry, translated by Katherine Woods, 1943.

DICKINSON   *The Complete Poems of Emily Dickinson* (**59**, **98**) by Emily Dickinson, edited by Thomas H. Johnson, 1960.

DONNE   "The Good Morrow" (**78**) by John Donne, in *Metaphysical Lyrics and Poems of the Seventeenth Century: Donne to Butler*, edited by Herbert J. C. Grierson, 1921.

DUNBAR   "Love's Apotheosis" (**156**), in *Lyrics of the Hearthside* by Paul Laurence Dunbar, 1899.

EATON   "Song of Psyyha" (**48**), in *Desire* by Charlotte Eaton, 1904.

ECCLESIASTES   Ecclesiastes 4:10-12 (**143**), New Revised Standard Version.

ELIOT   *Middlemarch: A Study of Provincial Life* (**121**) by George Eliot, 1900. *Adam Bede* (**127**) by George Eliot, 1859.

EMERSON   "Love" (**15**), in *Essays: First Series* by Ralph Waldo Emerson, 1841. *Early Poems of Ralph Waldo Emerson* (**25**) by Ralph Waldo Emerson, 1899.

EPHESIANS   Ephesians 5:28-31 (**24**), New Revised Standard Version.

ERNST   "A Father's Advice to His Daughter" (**102**). Used with permission of Dick Ernst.

ESKIMO LOVE SONG   Eskimo love song (**54**), in *Wedding Readings: Centuries of Writing and Rituals in Love and Marriage*, edited by Eleanor Munro, 1989.

FITZGERALD   *The Rubáiyát of Omar Khayyám* (**9**), translated by Edward FitzGerald, 1857.

FORSTER   *A Room with a View* (**16**) by E. M. Forster, 1908.

FORTNER   Selection (**166**) by William R. Fortner, in *Great Occasions: Readings for the Celebration of Birth, Coming-of-Age, Marriage, and Death*, edited by Carl Seaburg, 1998.

FRANKL   *Man's Search for Meaning: An Introduction to Logotherapy* (**4**, **143**) by Viktor Frankl, 1962.

FRIEDAN   *The Feminine Mystique* (**24**) by Betty Friedan, 1963.

FROMM   *The Art of Loving* (**17**, **90**, **114**) by Erich Fromm, 1956.

FULLER   "The Great Lawsuit. Man versus Men. Woman versus Women" (**139**) by Margaret Fuller, in *The Dial*, July 1843.

GANNETT   *The House Beautiful* (**9**, **95**, **107**) by William Channing Gannett, 1895.

GARRISON   "A Love Song" (**23**) by Theodosia Garrison, in *The Second Book of Modern Verse*, edited by Jessie B. Rittenhouse, 1922.

GIBRAN   "On Love" (**114**), in *The Prophet* by Kahlil Gibran, 1923.

GILBERT   "We Are, Therefore, We Love" (**22**), "We Meet on Holy Ground" (**34**), and "Loneliness and Love" (**137**), in *In the Holy Quiet of This Hour* by Richard S. Gilbert, 1995.

GREELEY   "A Wedding Prayer" (**39**) by Dana McLean Greeley, in *Great Occasions: Readings for the Celebration of Birth, Coming-of-Age, Marriage, and Death*, edited by Carl Sandburg, 1998. Used with permission of Faith Greeley Scovel.

HAMILTON-HOLWAY   "Freedom to Marry" (**37**) and "Go Now in Peace" (**44**). Used with permission of Barbara Hamilton-Holway.

HARDIES   "Contra Dancing" (**113**). Used with permission of Robert Hardies.

HAWTHORNE   Letter (**51**), by Nathaniel Hawthorne to Sophia Peabody, December 1839, in *Nathaniel Hawthorne and His Wife*, vol. 1, by Julian Hawthorne, 1884.

HECATON OF RHODES   Selection (**97**) by Hecaton of Rhodes, in *Wedding Readings: Centuries of Writing and Rituals on Love and Marriage*, edited by Eleanor Munro, 1989.

HÉLOISE   Letter (**23**) by Héloïse in *The World's Greatest Letters: From Ancient Greece to the Twentieth Century*, edited by Michelle Lovric, 2004.

HERBERT   "Love (III)" (**132**) by George Herbert, in *The Temple: Sacred Poems and Private Ejaculations*, edited by N. Ferrar, 1633.

HEYWARD   *Our Passion for Justice: Images of Power, Sexuality, and Liberation* (**7**) by Carter Heyward, 1984.

HOOD   "I Love Thee" (**71**), in *The Poetical Works of Thomas Hood* by Thomas Hood, date unknown.

HOPKINS   "At the Wedding March" (**32**), in *Poems* by Gerard Manley Hopkins, 1918.

HOYT   "The Lover Sings of a Garden" (**67**) by Helen Hoyt, in *The New Poetry*, edited by Harriet Monroe, 1917.

HUBBARD   *White Hyacinths* (**18**, **54**) by Elbert Hubbard, 1907.

HUBBELL   "Love Stories" (**5**). Used with permission of Phyllis Hubbell.

JEFFERYS   "We Have Lived and Loved Together" (**153**) by Charles Jefferys, in *The Best Loved Poems of the American People*, edited by Hazel Felleman, 1936.

JENKINS   "Love Autumnal" (**164**) by Oliver Jenkins, in *Anthology of Massachusetts Poets*, edited by William Stanley Brathwaite, 1922.

JOHNSON   "To Celia" (**68**) by Ben Johnson, in *The Golden Treasury of the Best Songs and Lyrical Poems in the English Language*, edited by Francis T. Palgrave, 1875.

JONG   "Cornucopia" (**133**), in *How to Save Your Own Life* by Erica Jong, 1977. Reprinted with permission of Erica Jong.

JOSEPH   "The Sun Has Burst the Sky" (**62**). Copyright © Jenny Joseph, *Selected Poems*, Bloodaxe, 1992. Johnson & Alcock EIN: 98-0201104.

KALIDASA   Selection (**35**) attributed to Kalidasa, in *Singing the Living Tradition*, 1993.

KEATS   Letter (**169**) by John Keats to Fanny Brawne, in *Wedding Readings: Centuries of Writing and Rituals on Love and Marriage*, edited by Eleanor Munro, 1989.

KIRSCHNER   Used with permission of Joseph Kirschner (**82**).

KITCHELL   *God's Dog: Conversations with Coyote* (**34**) by Webster Kitchell, 1991. Used with permission of author.

KOWALSKI   "Valentines" (**101**), in *Green Mountain Spring and Other Leaps of Faith* by Gary A. Kowalski, 1997. Used with permission of author.

KRAUSS   *The History of Love* (**65**) by Nicole Krauss, 2005.

LANDVIK   *Patty Jane's House of Curl* (**17**) by Lorna Landvik, 1995.

LAWRENCE   *Lady Chatterley's Lover* (**155**) by D. H. Lawrence, 1928.

LEAR   "The Owl and the Pussycat" (**50**), in *Nonsense Books* by Edward Lear, 1894.

L'ENGLE   *The Two-Part Invention: The Story of a Marriage* (**91**) by Madeleine L'Engle, 1988. *The Irrational Season* (**107**) by Madeleine L'Engle, 1977.

LEVERTOV   "The Ache of Marriage" (**87**), in *O Taste and See* by Denise Levertov. Copyright © 1964 by Denise Levertov. Reprinted with the permission of New Directions Publishing Corporation and Pollinger, Ltd. and the proprietor.

LINDBERGH   *Gifts from the Sea* (**88**) by Anne Morrow Lindbergh, 1991.

LIPPMANN   *A Preface to Morals* (**118**) by Walter Lippmann, 1957.

LOVELACE   "To Althea, from Prison" (**22**) by Richard Lovelace, in *The Oxford Book of English Verse: 1250-1900*, edited by Arthur Quiller-Couch, 1919.

LOWELL   "Opal" (**58**) by Amy Lowell, in *The Independent*, August 1916. "A Decade" (**159**) by Amy Lowell, in Chimera, May 1916.

LOWELL   "My Love" (**163**) by James Russell Lowell, in *The Golden Treasury of American Songs and Lyrics*, edited by Frederic Lawrence Knowles, date unknown.

LYNCH   *Bodies in Motion and at Rest: On Metaphor and Mortality* (**128**) by Thomas Lynch, 2000.

MACLEISH   "Poem in Prose" (**55**), in *Collected Poems, 1917-1982* by Archibald MacLeish. Copyright © 1985 by The Estate of Archibald MacLeish. Reprinted with the permission of Houghton Mifflin Company. All rights reserved.

MARKANDAYA   *Nectar in a Sieve* (**169**) by Kamala Markandaya, 1954.

MASTEN   "Words Are Just Words" (**69**), and "Let It Be a Dance" (**111**), in *Let It Be a Dance: Words and One-Liners.* "His and Hers" (**94**). Used with permission of Ric Masten.

MASTERS   "Mary McNeely" (**18**), in *Spoon River Anthology* by Edgar Lee Masters, 1916.

MATTHEWS   "Misgivings" (**125**) from *After All: Last Poems* by William Matthews. Copyright © 1998 by the Estate of William Matthews. Reprinted by permission of Houghton Mifflin Company. All rights reserved.

MCLEOD   Selections (**122**) by Irene Rutherford McLeod, in *Modern British Poetry*, edited by Louis Untermeyer, 1920.

MEREDITH   Excerpt from "Acid Test: Advice to My Son" (**171**), in *Hunter's Moon: Poems from Boyhood to Manhood* by Joseph Meredith. Copyright © 1993 by Time Being Books. Reprinted by permission.

MIKELSON   "Three Elements of Complete Love" (**141**). Used with permission of Thomas Mikelson.

MO-TSE   Selection (**4**) by Mo-Tse, in *Singing the Living Tradition*, 1993.

MONROE   "Love Song" (**53**) by Harriet Monroe, in *The New Poetry: An Anthology*, edited by Harriet Monroe, 1917.

MOORE   *Care of the Soul: A Guide for Cultivating Depth and Sacredness in Everyday Life* (**97**) by Thomas Moore, 1992.

MOORE   *Irish Melodies* (**166**), by Thomas Moore, 1834.

MORLEY   "The Wedded Lover" (**162**), in *Chimney Smoke* by Christopher Morley, 1921.

MORRIS   Selection (**16**) by William Morris, in *The Oxford Book of English Verse, 1250-1900*, edited by Arthur Quiller-Couch, 1919.

MOYERS   *The Power of Myth* (**109**) by Joseph Campbell and Bill Moyers, 1988.

Murdoch   *The Book and the Brotherhood* (**59**) by Iris Murdoch, 1987. *The Black Prince* (**64**) by Iris Murdoch, 1973.

Murfin   "Merlin Said" (**3**), in *We Build Temples in the Heart: Side by Side We Gather* by Patrick Murfin, 2004.

Navajo Night Chant   Navajo night chant (**36**), in *Poetry of the American West: A Columbia Anthology*, edited by Alison Hawthorne Deming, 1996.

Nerburn   *Letters to My Son: A Father's Wisdom on Manhood, Life, and Love* (**8**) by Kent Nerburn, 1994.

Neruda   "Sonnet 57" (**56**), in *One Hundred Love Sonnets* by Pablo Neruda, translated by Stephen Mitchell, 1960.

Nietzsche   Selection (**160**) by Friedrich Nietzsche, in *The Sun*, November 2005.

Olds   "Topography" (**83**), in *The Gold Cell* by Sharon Olds. Copyright © 1987 by Sharon Olds. Reprinted with the permission of Alfred A. Knopf, a division of Random House, Inc.

O'Reilly   "A White Rose" (**73**) by John Boyle O'Reilly, in *The Oxford Book of English Verse: 1250-1900*, edited by Arthur Quiller-Couch, 1919.

Osborne   *Look Back in Anger* (**104**) by John Osborne, 1957.

Parker   Selection (**161**) by Theodore Parker, in *Great Occasions: Readings for the Celebration of Birth, Coming-of-Age, Marriage, and Death*, edited by Carl Seaburg, 1998.

Patchen   "There Is Nothing False in Thee" (**74**) by Kenneth Patchen, in *Wedding Readings: Centuries of Writings and Rituals on Love and Marriage*, edited by Eleanor Munro, 1989.

PEATTIE   *The Basic Axiom of Marital Felicity* (**88**) by Donald Culross Peattie, date unknown.

PENN   Letter (**167**) by William Penn to Guilielma Maria Penn, in *Old Portraits and Modern Sketches* by John Greenleaf Whittier, date unknown.

PERRIN   "That Love May Grow" (**103**) and "Touch Me" (**140**), in *Prairie Smoke* by Melinda Morris Perrin, 2004. Used with permission of the author.

PIPHER   "Marriage" (**117**), in *Letters to a Young Therapist* by Mary Pipher, 2003.

POE   "The Bells" (**31**) by Edgar Allan Poe, in *The Yale Book of American Verse*, edited by Thomas R. Lounsbury, 1912.

PORTER   "Marriage Is Belonging" (**112**), in *Katherine Anne Porter: The Collected Essays and Occasional Writings*, by Katherine Anne Porter, 1970.

POUND   "The River-Merchant's Wife: A Letter" (**158**) by Ezra Pound, translated from Li Po, in *The New Poetry: An Anthology*, edited by Harriet Monroe, 1917.

PRATHER   *Love and Courage* (**152**) by Hugh Prather, 2001. Used with permission of Conari Press, imprint of Red Wheel/Weiser, Newburyport, MA, and San Francisco, CA. To order, please call 1-800-423-7087.

RICH   "Women and Honor: Some Notes on Lying," (**138**), in *Arts of the Possible: Essays and Conversations* by Adrienne Rich, 2001.

RILKE   *Letters to a Young Poet* (**8**, **87**) by Rainer Maria Rilke, translated by Kent Nerburn, 2000.

ROHDE   "The Blessings of Age" (**89**), in *In the Simple Morning Light* by Barbara Rohde, 1994. Used with permission of Kermit Rohde.

ROSSETTI   "A Birthday" (**20**), in *Goblin Market and Other Poems* by Christina Rossetti, 1862. "The First Day" (**64**) by Christina Rossetti, in *A Book of Love Poetry,* edited by Jon Stallworthy, 1974.

ROSSETTI   "Sudden Light" (**168**), in *Poems: An Offering to Lancashire* by Dante Gabriel Rossetti, 1863.

RUSSELL   *Marriage and Morals* (**99**) by Bertrand Russell.

RUTH   Ruth 1:16-17 (**122**), King James Version.

SANDBURG   "Playthings of the Wind" (**32**) and "Old-fashioned Requited Love" (**89**), in *Smoke and Steel* by Carl Sandburg, 1920. "Joy" (**39**) by Carl Sandburg, in *The New Poetry: An Anthology,* edited by Harriet Monroe, 1917.

SCAFIDI   "Prayer for a Marriage" (**169**), in *Sparks from a Nine-Pound Hammer: Poems* by Steve Scafidi. Copyright © 2001. Reprinted by permission of Louisiana State University Press.

SCHATZ   "Freedom to Love" (**9**). Used with permission of Daniel Schatz.

SCOTT   *The Lay of the Last Minstrel* (**17**) by Sir Walter Scott, 1805.

SEARL   "Always a Beginning" (**41**), in *A Place of Your Own* by Edward Searl, 1998. "Love Poem" (**69**).

SHAKER HYMN   Shaker hymn (**10**) in *Wedding Readings: Centuries of Writing and Rituals on Love and Marriage,* edited by Eleanor Munro, 1989.

SHAKESPEARE   *Hamlet* (**49**), *Romeo and Juliet* (**73**), "Sonnet 18" (**75**), "Sonnet 116" (**139**), in *The Oxford Shakespeare: The Complete Works of William Shakespeare* by William Shakespeare, edited by W. J. Craig, 1914.

SHAW   Preface (**104**), in *Getting Married* by George Bernard Shaw, 1911.

SHERMAN   "Love's Springtide" (**77**) by Frank Dempster Sherman, in *The Little Book of Modern Verse*, edited by T. Rittenhouse, 1917.

SHIELDS   *Unless* (**160**) by Carol Shields, 2002.

SHIPLEY   "I Am the Song of Love" (**5**) by Joseph T. Shipley, in *Poetica Erotica: A Collection of Rare and Curious Amatory Veres*, edited by T. R. Smith, 1931.

SIBR   "Sanctification" (**33**). Used with permission of Carolyn Sibr.

SIDNEY   Selection (**130**) by Sir Philip Sidney, in *A Book of Love Poetry*, edited by Jon Stallworthy, 1974.

SMILEY   *At Paradise Gate* (**141**) by Jane Smiley, 1981.

SNYDER   "Love and Loss" (**96**). Used with permission of Joshua Snyder.

SOUTHERN   "I Do, I Do" (**136**). Used with permission of Vanessa Southern.

STODDARD   Selection (**165**) by Richard Henry Stoddard, in *The Yale Book of American Verse*, edited by Thomas R. Lounsbury, 1912.

STONE AND BLACKWELL   "The Protest of Lucy Stone and Henry Blackwell Upon Their Marriage on May 2, 1855" (**92**) by Lucy Stone and Henry Blackwell, in *Lucy Stone: Pioneer of Women's Rights* by Alice Stone Blackwell, 1930.

STRAUSS   "Should Marriage Be Saved?" (**127**). Used with permission of Lynn Strauss.

TAYLOR   Used with permission of Alan Taylor (**102**).

TEASDALE   "Gifts" (**14**), selection (**47**), "Faults" (**58**), "Peace" (**123**), and "After Parting" (**138**), in *Love Songs* by Sara Teasdale, 1917.

THOREAU   "Friendship" (**167**) by Henry David Thoreau, in *The Book of Love*, edited by Andrew M. Greeley and Mary G. Durkin, 2002.

TRUEBLOOD   "Prayer" (**29**), in *I Was Alive—And Glad* by Roscoe Trueblood, date unknown. Used with permission of First Parish Unitarian Universalist in Cohasset, Massachusetts.

TYUTCHEV   "Last Love" (**154**) by Fyodor Tyutchev, translated by Vladimir Nabokov, in *A Book of Love Poetry*, edited by Jon Stallworthy, 1973.

VAN GOGH   Letter (**12**) by Vincent Van Gogh to Theo Van Gogh, November 1878, transcribed from exhibit at the Metropolitan Museum of Art, New York.

WATTS   "Vision" (**11**) by May Theilgaard Watts, in *Love's Witness: Five Centuries of Love Poetry* by Women, edited by Jill Hollis, 1993.

WHITMAN   Selections (**12**, **49**, **165**) and "Song of the Open Road" (**105**), in *Leaves of Grass* by Walt Whitman, 1900.

WILCOX   "Friendship After Love" (**149**) by Ella Wheeler Wilcox, in *American Poetry: The Nineteenth Century*, vol. 2, date unknown.

WILKINSON   "A Woman's Beloved" (**130**) by Marguerite Wilkinson, in *The New Poetry: An Anthology*, edited by Harriet Monroe, 1917.

WILLIAMS   *The Velveteen Rabbit* (**90**) by Margery Williams, 1922.

WILLIAMS   "This Is Just to Say" (**118**), in *Collected Poems: 1909-1939*, vol. 1, by William Carlos Williams, edited by Christopher MacGowan. Copyright 1938 by New Directions Publishing Corporation. Reprinted with the permission of New Directions Publishing Corporation and Carcanet Press, Ltd.

Wilson   Letter (**52**) from Woodrow Wilson to Edith Wilson, September 1883, on PBS American Experience website.

Wyatt   "To F. W." (**147**) by Edith Wyatt, in *The New Poetry: An Anthology*, edited by Harriet Monroe, 1917.

Yeats   "The Wild Swans at Coole" (**10**), in *Solomon to Sheba* by William Butler Yeats, 1919. "A Drinking Song" (**38**), in *Responsibilities and Other Poems* by William Butler Yeats, 1916. "He Wishes for the Cloths of Heaven" (**124**), in *The Wind Among the Reeds* by William Butler Yeats, 1899. Selection (**163**) by William Butler Yeats, in *Oxford Book of English Verse: 1250-1900*, edited by Arthur Quiller-Couch, 1919.